MW01435471

The Tears of Haiti

THE TEARS OF HAITI

Louisket Edmond

Professional Instructor in French & Spanish in Connecticut & Former Assistant Professor at University of Maine

Copyright © 2010 by Louisket Edmond.

Library of Congress Control Number:		2010908468
ISBN:	Hardcover	978-1-4535-1769-7
	Softcover	978-1-4535-1768-0
	Ebook	978-1-4535-1770-3

All rights reserved. No part of this book may be reproduced or transmitted in any form or by any means, electronic or mechanical, including photocopying, recording, or by any information storage and retrieval system, without permission in writing from the copyright owner.

This book was printed in the United States of America.

To order additional copies of this book, contact:
Xlibris Corporation
1-888-795-4274
www.Xlibris.com
Orders@Xlibris.com
81952

Contents

Preface 11
Haitian Teacher Of Birth 17
Home-schooling Education in Haiti 19
Child's Experiences and Education in Haiti 22
Childhood Experiences and Education in Haiti 29
Childhood Beating Stories 31
Overthrow Aristide Regime 40
Haiti was Born with Tears 43
Running for Representative to the Haitian Congress 51
Legislative and Municipal Elections on May 21, 2000 60
Final Goodbye to Haiti 62
Hungry for an Education in the U.S.A 68
Minorities in Haiti and in the USA 90
Haitian's survivors on Jan 12, 2010 92

To my parents, who taught me not to limit myself
To Nagena, who taught me the real life
To Ludgi, who taught me to smile
To Louidnie & Lovelie, who taught me to love
And to the memory of 300,000 people who lost their lives in the powerful Earthquake on January 12, 2010 in the western part of the island of Hispaniola.

Haiti has been crying since her birth

Poem written by Louisket Edmond
A black life doesn't cost a lot in Haiti/Un noir ne coûte pas chère en Haiti
La vi yon moun nwe pa koute anpil kob an ayiti/ La vida de un negro no vale tanto en la isla haitiana
Omelette à Oaxaca, Mexique / Omelette in Oaxaca, Mexico

Preface

Brief History of Haiti:

The slaves brought from Africa to the island of Hispaniola, enriched this part of the world through many years of vigorous suffering. Slave masters, in compliance with European colonizers, blessed the slave market, in the new world, black race in slavery fought for its own Independence, which was achieved in 1804. In Haiti for 219 Years Bois-Caiman has been a very sacred high place for most Haitian voodooists, who believed that their religion could coexist with one of the major religions of Western Hemisphere today and her children have been crying in every corner around the world. Two year after the French revolution, the African slaves stood up to free the western part of the island from their French and English Masters since then The Pearl of The Antilles has become a land of great suffering, misery and political Tensions, antagonism and instability. As a result, Haiti is one of the poorest countries in the world.

In the afternoon of January 12, 2010, a powerful earthquake hit the island of Hispaniola. As you know, many people were killed, perhaps as many as 300.000 and millions of others have been injured. All the infrastructure of the Haitian capital has been destroyed: The national palace, schools, churches, parliament, Toussaint Louverture International Airport, hospitals, hotels, etc . . .

The situation remains serious in the western part of the island. The news is about the dead missing and about miraculous survivals in Haiti. Our faith is still alive fellow Haitians and we need to stand up in this difficult time to help those unfortunate people still on the island to receive not only food, water and shelter, but also education. It is a necessity for our future leaders. Think about those who were asked to pull bodies from debris, Haitians and foreigners who were buried without coffins, Haitians who lost their legs, and live on the streets. Also, think about some of the survivors who were unable to breathe due to the smell of the dead and the debris in the western part of the island. Can we still believe that anyone life doesn't cost a lot after the powerful quake which made the world cry regardless of race, religion, national origin, and gender?

Island Of Hispaniola

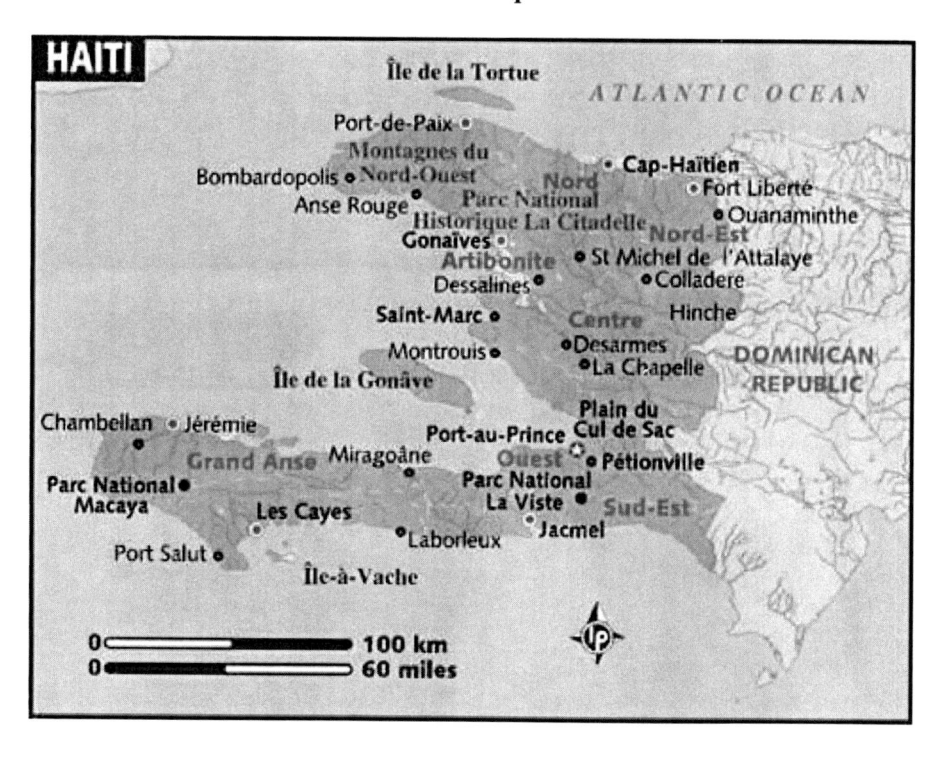

The Bible teaches that God will bring about these changes on the earth.

> "He will wipe out every tear from their eyes, and death will be no more, neither will mourning nor outcry nor pain be anymore."—Revelation 21: 4

Our great Brother Jesus Christ said: "Keep on asking, and it will be given you; keep on seeking, and you will find; keep on knocking, and it will be opened to you."—Matthew 7: 7.

Haitian Teacher Of Birth

I just finished talking to the person who gave me life, my mother. She told me that I was born on a day and season when leaves and flowers started blooming in La Gonave, an island to the west of the capital city, Port-au-Prince, Haiti. Two years before I was born a dictator named Jeanclaude (Baby Doc) Duvalier was sworn in at the National Palace of Haiti as president for life.

Before I started writing my story based on my experiences in Haiti and in the United States of America, I called my mother and thanked her. Some of my experiences are set in misery, while others are normal things that happen in everyday life. My mother named me Louisket Edmond after my father, Isidor Edmond. My grandfather was a blue collar worker who died young, and my father became an orphan at the age of 10 in La Gonave.

Most people who knew my grandfather Romulus Edmond told me that he was a talented man with a great character. When I was growing up in Haiti, my life was similar to the lives of millions of Haitian children who go to bed hungry without three meals per day, or clean water. Without the opportunity to attend school at an early age and without health insurance life was a challenge. I was born in a village which is located about three miles from the main town on the island of La Gonave. There was no road, no running water or electricity, no school, no church, no nurse and no doctor. To be born in these circumstances only means that one's chances are limited. How do you make your life meaningful without education or preserve it without clean water?

On a beautiful day in December 1979 when I was six years old, my mother tried to explain to me, how she gave birth to me in my grandparents' house because the village where she lived had a population of 400 people with no hospital. The Haitian government with its limited resources has not provided basic infrastructures for the children or for the entertainment of visitors and residents of this village of Fregate in La Gonave. My mother remained calm while telling me her story with a cranky voice that I could not understand. She said, "Louisket", and I hesitated when she called me by my first name because she usually called me by my last name.

It took her more than two minutes to add another word. I have forgotten about playing with my younger brother Jony who kept calling me while my mother was talking to me. I focused on my mother, on what she was saying, she told me that during her pregnancy she got sick and she did not have any prenatal care because the whole island of La Gonave had a long history of isolation. In spite of nine months of sorrow, she thought that the last day would be easier or better, she was tired of crying, tired of walking in the dark since the village of Fregate did not have electricity, she was tired of carrying me in her womb for nine months, she did not have a doctor or midwife who could help her with information for taking care of me.

My mother told me about my grandmother, Louicia Denival, the mother of my father, who died in the childbirth along with baby, after her husband Romulus Edmond was buried no more than a month before. Nine children were left orphaned and in misery. My father Isidor Edmond was one of them.

I felt terrified when I learned this story about my grandparents. It was obvious to me ever at that young age that the Haitian system was not functional. I cried my mother tried to stop me from crying and I cried out. I was imagining how nine children would survive after losing their parents who really loved and cared for them. I was too young to learn this story. It was a very sad situation for me personally and I realized why my first name was Louisket, after my grandmother Louicia, who died while giving birth to a beautiful child. I was thinking recently about the dictator François Duvalier, who was president for life at the time, stealing the Haitian peoples' money, killing them in order to have power, while my grandmother Louicia wanted to have only one thing, not to be a president, nor a prime minister, or senator, all she wanted was a nurse, or a doctor who could have helped her in giving birth to an innocent child.

What this story shows me is the link between corruption and lives of ordinary people; corruption is immoral, illegal, but also a way of destroying many lives. If the Haitian government authorities used their resources to build roads, public buildings, health centers, and so on, my grandmother wouldn't have died along with her child, and the nine children she left behind would have had a better life.

My mother continued her story another time by telling me how she suffered when she carried me during nine months of her pregnancy; she had only one fear that she would lose me and die herself like my grandmother who died during her last childbirth. Nevertheless, I was born after a long painful period, one morning on May 13, 1973. My parents were so excited to have a boy, since they already had a girl named Ifrancia. Now they needed to work harder in order to take care of both their children.

Home-schooling Education in Haiti

Most expects in early education agree that Preschool education is one of the most important gifts a parent can give a child in his lifetime. It is different from all later educational. It helps the child to have a good foundation and grow socially and intellectually in a good society. In today's society people talk about daycare services, after school programs, and kindergarden. Those options were not available growing up in Haiti in the countryside about three miles outside of the small town of Anse-à-galets, La Gonave. Therefore, my mother's options were to move us to Anse-à-galets' school or let my sister and I stay in the house to attend home-schooling in the village. La Gonave is an island about 42 miles long, 9 miles wide, and covers an area of 243 square miles.

So my sister, I francia, and I attended home schooling with a man named Louiner Fils-Aimé who called himself "directeur" in French (Principal in English). According to my father, he was a man who received a high school education in a Catholic school in Montrouis. Montrouis was located a few miles from where my mother used to buy her merchandises for the work she did at home. However, people needed to take a boat from LaGonave in order to go to Montrouis, so "le directeur" came to our home.

My sister Ifrancia was seven years old and I was five years old and we were not allowed to attend a regular school, because it was too far away from our neighborhood. We had to stay in our parent's house and Mr. Fils-Aimé came to teach us every morning at six a.m. because other kids were waiting for him to teach later. It was the way the kids were taught in the countryside in Haiti. One morning, Mr. Fils-Aimé came to the house and taught us how to read and write. He used the direct method to make my sister better understand the French alphabet. He read some words twice while we both were listening to him and after that he asked my sister to read by herself. Finally, he called me and I did what he told me to do. I always responded to his questions correctly. When he gave us a report card, most of the time I got a better grade than my sister, who was born two years before me. Our teacher liked me a lot. There was no technology at the time in my area. We had to memorize everything by heart otherwise the dictator Jean Claude (Baby Doc) Duvalier's regime gave teachers full power to beat students when they didn't follow instructions. Sometimes, Mr. Fils-Aimé hit both of us with a belt if we didn't review or memorize his notes, but this was not too bad compared to the experience I was going to have later.

My mother helped my sister and me to do our assignments from the home schooling. She taught us that the best way to memorize the lessons was to keep our books all the time and not play if we did not finish preparing our homework. Before going to bed, I had to count from one to fifty, and a year later from fifty to hundred in French. Also religious beliefs played a big role in our society.

As a child, I had to pray to God out loud every night, even though I didn't really know who God was while my parents were listening, I prayed. "Leve vwa w ", said my mother in Creole (meaning "raised your voice.")

I prayed by raising my voice without hesitation and I enjoyed it whereas my sister was afraid of praying loudly in public or private. It's like I was older than her. Sometimes, I told her if you gave me a big plate of food, I would pray twice for you and me. Our mother urged both of us not to pray at the same time just to make sure both of us learned how to pray to God.

Besides praying, my sister knew how to cook very well and she was the boss of cooking in the house. If I were not nice to her, when my mother went out to market, she would not give me enough food, and she tried to punish me. When my mother came back to the house, I told her what my sister did and she would give me more food. In Haiti, most of the time, the person who cooked would distribute the meal since people came from all over the countryside and there was not enough to let everyone take their own amount. Then I had multiple reasons to please my sister all the time as she became the chief of cooking. When kids play together, sometimes they fight with each other and that happened between me and my sister. When I got a better grade than her, I told her that she didn't know anything and that caused a problem. She got mad and tried to beat me. Most of the time, I ran away because in my culture the older child had the right to beat the younger no matter what happened. I wouldn't have equality with my sister. I knew that because my mother taught me that I should respect my sister all the time in whatever circumstances. The entire childish thing changed when my sister and I got older. Now I show her my true love and respect.

In any case, my own experience as a child in Haiti was heavy and depressing. The lack of social infrastructure: inadequate roads, school, medical services, water systems, and so on, made me suffer and grow too fast as a child.

I believe the ultimate causes of Haiti's misery are human ignorance, rather than malace, and it is a controversial topic as well, which may take a life to overcome. It is also a difficult thing for my students in Camden, New Jersey; Miami, Florida; Orono, Maine; and Winsted, Connecticut; to understand and along with the world since they were born outside of Haiti. Haiti has been covered by tears and every Haitian was all tears, but quiet. Whereas I learned from my former teachers that silence is the death and I wanted this misery to end. Haitians needed to wake up and demand more to ensure a better future.

After two years of home schooling, my parents believed at the age of 7 that I could walk to a regular school, which was located about three miles from my parent's house. There were so many children on the streets, playing soccer unable to have home schooling or to attend a regular school. Most of those children lived in my neighborhood and some were working on the plantations and became breeders who never went to school. It wasn't like they didn't want to know how to read and write in French, but their parents were so poor that they couldn't afford the tutors or the tuitions. My parents weren't rich; they were struggling to survive as thousands of Haitians were. However, they believed in education and they knew the real change could have come from knowledge. They were very motivated and sacrificed themselves for me and my sister to get a formal education.

Child's Experiences and Education in Haiti

At the beginning of 1980, my parents had two more children, Jony Edmond and Kettelie. The United States of America welcomed all foreigners, especially Cubans and Haitians, to do the jobs the American people didn't want to do. My father was a member of the National Security Volunteer who was created by François (Papa Doc) Duvalier, a well educated doctor, authoritarian leader, dictator, who called himself a president for life. Papa Doc was scared of the Haitian military that had a tradition of overthrowing the former presidents. In order to consolidate his power, he used all the peasants by giving them a little power while misappropriating international aid money or transferring those funds to his personal accounts. Even though Papa Doc died in 1971 in Haiti, his son Jean Claude (Baby Doc) Duvalier, still a teenager, and law student without experience, succeeded his father upon his death. Baby Doc became the youngest leader in the world and had a big responsibility to feed and educate more than 6 million poor people in the Caribbean. As a young leader, he witnessed what his father had done in Haiti and made some reforms, but the regime remained mostly the same. He released some political prisoners and kept the rural militia members who didn't have any official salary and looked for money in drugs, or abused the Haitian people. After less than a decade, the Haitian professionals were very intimidated by the Baby Doc regime and looked for other opportunities outside of Haiti. Some well educated professionals fled the island of Hispaniola to several Latin-Americans countries, and to Brooklyn, New York; Miami, Florida; Boston, Massachusetts in the United States of America. They also emigrated to French-speaking countries in Europe, Africa, especially those that had a lack of teachers and doctors at the time, since most of their colonizers left. Many African people won their independence in the early 1960's. Therefore the African continent needed the Haitians, especially those who shared the French language and culture. Some Haitian professionals became members of United Nations agencies to escape from persecution and went to Africa to work.

Other Haitians risked their lives by fleeing flimsy over crowded boats in order to look for a better life outside of Haiti. Some people spent seven to ten days before arriving in Miami, Florida, or Bahamas. If the boat reached American soil at the time, all those boat people were welcome and the American authorities just transported them to the hospital for treatment after ten days of starving. My father was one of them who risked his life on the sea in order to live the American dream and make me a teacher in the United States of America.

I remember now a great American Nobel Peace Prize winner, and I must thank him. A former peanut farmer, Senator, Governor, the 39th President of the United States of America, who welcomed the Haitian people, and most importantly my father, here in the United States of America. I c wouldn't be a teacher today in this great country if three decades ago President James Earl "Jimmy "Carter, Jr didn't allow my father to stay here. When the Haitian dictator Baby Doc was abusing his own people, President Carter gave them the opportunity to the pursuit of life, liberty, and happiness in the country of Georges Washington. When the Haitian people were crying in Haiti for food, clean water, security, no corruptions, the 39th President of the United States of America heard their voices and he said, "no more tears for Haitians". President Carter, I just want to say "thank you for allowing thousand Haitians and especially my father to live the American dream," you saved many lives. Live a long life and May God bless your country.

Also, I haven't forgotten Senator Ted Kennedy who was one of the longest-serving members of the United States Congress. He spent more than four decades in the U.S. Senate and fought for civil rights, education, and immigration reform, equality for minorities, women, the disabled and gay Americans. Senator Ted Kennedy didn't like injustice. During his career he worked very hard to improve life in the United States of America and saved many lives around the world, unfortunately he didn't live to see the health care reform for uninsured people in the United States. Senator Kennedy, we know that you have left us in the struggle, but you are alive each time we think about the misery of our countries, each time we send money to our family members and friends, each time we get sick and don't have insurance. We will continue to remember you for life and peace for your soul.

Before sending me to the regular school for the first time at the age of seven, my parents argued and were divided. My mother told my dad that he had four children to take care of and he had to stop working for the Haitian regime.

And look for a better life for his family abroad, not in Haiti. According to my father, he changed his name to Tonton Macoute for the safety of his family, not because he wanted to. It was the only way to protect the family members he would leave behind otherwise they might get beaten or killed by the Duvalier military.

My father disagreed with my mother and didn't want to leave his four children and her behind in order to look for a new life away from them. He was an orphan who didn't have enough affection from his parents since they both died when he was ten. He spent most of his time with an uncle who abused him. He was overworked, malnourished, beaten by his uncle. Finally, he had a family, wife and four children who cared about him, who put love in his heart and made him feel whole. "How was I going to survive without them", said my father, "in a foreign country?" Indeed, he didn't know where he was going. According to him, many people tried to reach the American soil by boat, but they died because their boat sank after several days on the sea. "Chèche lavi men detwi lavi" in Haitian Creole meant "look for life but destroys it." I understand that my father not only he cared about us, but he was also afraid of dying.

My mother was named Elitane Petion, a descendent of the former president Alexander Petion who he had a good education in France and became one of the founders of the republic of Haiti.

My mother was dissatisfied with the Duvalier regime. Since my father didn't think about the future of her children in a country where people lived under $ 1.00 a day, she said to my father, "You know, I ought to leave you my skirt and you can stay here like a girl in Haiti with our children, and then I will take your jeans in order to ensure the future of our children in the United States of America". My mother was very smart and she believed in this powerful country. She was very motivated to risk her life for me along with my sisters and brothers.

Finally, my father chose to be a man, and leave us even if he died. He became a brave and courageous father. He left the house March 16, 1980 with tears in his eyes and he went to Zetwa, a small town which was located on the coast two and half miles from our village. According to my father, the sailboat left the wharf on March 18, 1980 in the afternoon with 140 people onboard and arrived in Miami, Florida on March 28, 1980 after ten days on the sea. The name of the sailboat was "Tibourik" in Haitian it means "little donkey." There was another sailboat named "Tibato" or "little boat," which left the port with 200 people about the same time. They got lost and arrived on a desert island not too far from Guantamo, but they thought that it was Miami, Florida. Everybody got off the sailing boat at night and started looking for people on a desert island. When it became daylight, the boat people realized that wasn't Miami, it was only a desert island. According to many survivors the boat disappeared. Nevertheless, hundreds of Haitians stayed on this dessert island without food, and water and they couldn't communicate with their relatives while there. After many days of starving, some of them ate herbs and three of them took to the sea floatiny on their bellis a piece of wood. According to Olvin Laguerre, a Haitian survivor, "I can't stay here on a desert island and starve without doing anything". He floated with the wood and spent two days on the sea without eating until some American fishermen rescued him and alerted the United States Coast Guard boat. His body was weak and he told the rescuers that he left a hundred Haitians on a desert island and two floating in the water. The American authorities sent food, clean water and medicine to those who were on a desert island. When they got to the island, they found most of the Haitians had died of starvation, but they transported the survivors to the hospital aboard the United States Coast Guard.

It was a sign that thousands of Haitians were in desperate need and that their country would not help them. It was a difficult time for my family in Haiti who didn't hear from my father. My mother got attacked by my father's sisters, who thought he had died and blamed her for forcing him to risk his life on the sea for a better life. We didn't know that my father had arrived in the United States. His sailboat didn't have anything problems, nobody died, but he couldn't call us since the houses in our village didn't have telephones. My mother cried in the morning, in the afternoon, and at night because gossips said that my father vomited a lot and the people on board threw him to the sea. I can see now how my aunts became angry with my mother for worrys about their brother.

My aunts came to my mother's house to find their brother even when they knew that my father wasn't there. Neighbors stood up all over my mother's yard to watch the scene.

My aunts wanted to fight with my mother for my father whom they thought had died. My sister cried and I cried too, but I didn't really know what I was crying for. However, the way my aunts were talking to my mother, I felt there was something wrong. My aunts said to my mother, "ou vle gen bel kay, ou voye Isidor al mouri nan lanmè," in Haitian Creole, "you want to have a nice house, you sent Isidor to die on the sea."

My mother, Elitane, met my father when she was seventeen years old. Her father Saint Jules Petion, moved in 1968 from Bois-de-Chaine to Fregate with his wife, Syltane Estiverne, along with eight children to the area where my father was born and raised. My grandfather Saint-Jules was an owner of a sailboat. He came to Fregate, according to him, in order to be close to his boat and to transport charcoal to Arcachaie or Saint-Marc. He was my best friend and he told me stories all the time. He used to live in Martinique, a French island in the Caribbean. Unfortunately, my grandfather died last year in Haiti.

According to my mother's birth certificate, my father was little bit older than her. He came to my grandmother's house every evening and shook the hands of my uncles, my grandfather and kissed my grandmother and aunts. It seemed certain that everyone liked my father before my mother fell in love with him. Two of my uncles, who were my father's best friends, gave him a tour of the house when he visited for the first time and later they played cards with him. But he was a shy young man, my mother said, and he never gave her a hug when people were around. Once they were alone, he always wanted several hugs from my mother while giving those hugs, my mother fell in love with him. Several months later, they were engaged. Their first child, a beautiful girl named Ifrancia Edmond, was born first.

After 9 years living together, they had 4 children. They should have controlled their love better to avoid having too many children, especially in a country where 80 percent of the population live under poverty lines. Yet, my parents were religious and they believed according to the Bible it was a sin to prevent having children.

After all, it wasn't like my mother wanted my father to risk his life on the sea. My father wasn't the only person who wanted to live the American dream, so did all this other people who accompanied him. If there had been enough jobs in Haiti and the regime of Duvalier wasn't intimidated its own people, my mother, wouldn't have asked my father to seek a better life in the United States of America.

I believe my mother is a visionary, a thinker who had a dream for her four children. She sacrificed herself, not having any hugs from her husband for a long while, and lived for many years for me, my younger brother and sisters. She didn't want us to stay in the misery of Haiti and die. She was ready to sacrifice her life on the sea in order for me to become graduate from the University of Maine in Orono. However, no one understood my mother at the time. She was a quiet hero who didn't have a big title. This is the pain of thousands of Haitian women who remained in Haiti for decades, while their husbands were looking for a better life illegally outside of Haiti. As a result of that, most of the Women died without seeing their husbands again after the men left the island, because they did not have documentation to return to their homeland.

My mother endured all kind of pain as a woman in Haiti. It is a loss in every way for a couple to live far from each other for many years. It's a little painful to talk about the strategies my mother used to help me become a real citizen today. She did a good job to encourage my father to come to the United States of America.

In any case, my aunts didn't see my mother's reasons and they only blamed her. It was time for my grandfather Saint-Jules to arrive in my parents' house to make my aunts stay away from my mother, and then for safety reasons, my grandfather moved all of us to his house.

I remember that my family members and friends kept coming to my grandfather's house after we got to his place and they talked to my mother about

God and prayed for all of us. They said that we needed to trust Jehovah Lord because He loved everyone and that my father might be alive. The religious groups tried to dry my mother's tears by quoting the Bible. They also encouraged her to attend special services where they could pray for her along with her family. The minister sang with his members in my grandfather's house "Bondye bon, Bondye bon, Bondye bon pou tout moun" in Haitian Creole meant "God is good, God is good, God is good for everybody."

It was one of the most difficult times in my childhood. It seemed everything was against my family. My sister and I had to stop the homeschooling because there was no peace in the house with our dear mother who kept crying for our father. The public opinion said that he died in the sea. We both wanted to interact with other kids, make new friends, not stay in our grandfather's house. However, my mother couldn't manage our education because of the loss of her love. Indeed, my sister wasn't interested to learn anything, anything in the house. She had mentioned a list of problems. For instance, she didn't think our home school teacher had a normal curriculum, a methodology of teaching, or nor did he understand that sometimes kids wanted to play and relax. He never gave us a break. She said to me that Mr. Fils aimé gave us too many assignments at once and wondered why he had to beat us for little mistakes. Then I had no choice but to back up my sister. I responded to her that Mr. Fils-Aimé was a bad teacher and I didn't like him. But in reality he wasn't a bad home teacher. As kids we wanted to go away from our grandfather's house and play on the road on the way to school. In other words, we needed our freedom as children.

While we were home schooled, I never saw any supervisor who could have observed Mr. Fils-Aimé when he was teaching us. No social worker, no blackboard, and no library. It was the way; the dictator Baby Doc ignored the children in the isolated regions, not only in LaGonave, but all over Haiti.

When kids received home schooling in Haiti at the time, it didn't mean that they were ill, but just the lack of educational infrastructure. The Haitian authorities did not care about children; they preferred to solve the overpopulation problem by moving people afraid and driving them to leave the island. Economic misery made the poor become poorer and the rich become richer.

After six months of sorrow and fears, my mother received a radio, six hundred dollars and a cassette. My father was alive; he talked to us and greeted every member of our family in the cassette. My aunts came to listen to my father's voice in my grandfather's house to ensure that it wasn't a lie, and they were very happy to have this good news. They forgot that it was my mother who forced my father to get to the United States of America. The way my aunts were acting it seemed they had never had a problem with my mother before. They kissed her and screamed that now they had a brother in the United States of America. That was a big achievement for an orphan to live the American dream. My father became famous among the people who had heard the good news that he was alive. They came to my grandfather's house from all over of the countryside just to listen to my father's voice. But my father explained in details what happened while acrossing the sea. There was no more food in the sailboat, no water after less than eight days after leaving Haiti. The people aboard were starving, some of them were crying, they wanted to eat, but there was no food, no water either.

It was a sad moment for all of us who were listening to the cassette. He added that they had a good captain who knew what he was doing even though it was the first time he acrossed the sea to Florida. He summarized also what he saw in the United States: lot of the big buildings, roads, electricity, schools, churches, jobs etc.

Instead of smiling, my mother was yelling while listening to my father's cassette. Was she thinking about my father's misery and how she was going to lose him? My uncles held her and asked her to calm down and my mother listened to them after a little while.

In a word, it was a victory for my family who was struggling to survive. It is wonderful to have a mother who was intelligent and cared for her children. There was no conflict between my mother and aunts anymore. My mother was free to return to our house. My aunts didn't intimidate her anymore. My grandfather advised her not to return to her house without my uncles in case of emergency and she agreed with her father. Now my uncles' Ugin Petion and Lucien Petion escorted us to the house. My life had changed with my father in the United States of America.

Childhood Experiences and Education in Haiti

In the fall of 1980 I was 7 years old and my sister Ifrancia was 9. We left the house to go to school for the first time. My mother decided to send us to school in Zetwa, a small town where we could have a better education than the home schooling. Since she learned our father was alive, she had peace in mind. It was about two miles and two hours or less depending how fast a child could walk.

By the way, my mother accompanied my sister and me to the school. She talked to the principal about us. After a little while she left us. I personally enjoyed the first day and I felt comfortable with the other kids. I made new friends the same day. I played soccer outside of the school with my new friends at eleven thirty am. because we had a free period. My mother gave me money; I bought a meal and shared it with my new friends. They liked me because I was an easy going attractive boy, and we have kept in touch with each other since then.

The first activity my new teacher asked the class to do was to introduce ourselves. I did it and she continued calling more than sixty names. She taught us how to count from one to ten, but I already knew this stuff. Now I thought about the home school teacher, Mr. Fils-Aimé who was patient with me and my sister, although we didn't admit that he did a great job for both of us. We were very smart among more than sixty students in our classroom. When the teacher called us to do something, we did it very well. Finally, once the class was done, my sister and I walked

The two hours back to the home. Upon arrival, we kissed our mother and visitors who were in the house.

"Koman sa te ye?", "said my mother in Creole"(How was it?) I immediately answered the question, it was great mother and I loved the children. The teacher taught us how to count and we sang in French. "Mwen kontan tande bon nouvel de lekol nou an," said my mother meaning she was glad to hear good news about our school, and it was time to charge our clothes and," come to eat," concluded my mother.

Each morning before going to school, I had to take care of the animals. My mother was a business woman who bought rice, beans, and corn in St-Marc and sold them for a profit in LaGonave; and my father was a farmer, a breeder who had a lot of animals including, goats, cows, donkeys, horses, dogs and cats. Since I was too young, my mother had someone else who took care of the cows, but the rest of the smaller animals were my responsibility because my father was away in the United States. Consequently, I rushed dinner and went to move the goats, donkeys, and horses into the forests. By the time, I got back to the house, the sun was already down. Remember there was no electricity in the countryside where I was living and I had to use a kerosene lamp in order to study for the next day. Otherwise, I was going to get beaten by my teacher. Tired or not I had to get my assignments done for at night and wake up early in the morning to take care of the animals.

That work was more than misery for a young child. Each time I relive my childhood, I cry. It isn't a memory of joy, but of sadness. As anyone can imagine, living a life with these feelings makes it impossible to regain totally control of my emotions. I learned from my father that bad memories stick better than good, and as a man, I have to fight for a better life until I leave this world.

Childhood Beating Stories

A new problem started several weeks later when my sister and I got to school late, with about fifteen other children whose parents were able to afford a private school at the time. We lived too far and were unable to get to school on time. The roads were very bad. Sometimes as a little boy I fell down on the roads and cried out. The older students came back and helped me to stand up and asked me to stop crying. One day we were about ten minutes late by the time we got to the school. The superintendent hit all of us with a belt, but he knew for a fact where we came from and that we had to walk a long way in order to get to his school. However, he didn't care about us and he had the power to do anything to us. There were no children protecting laws under the Jean Claude (Baby Doc) Duvalier regime. Beating a child in school was normal. As a result of that many school teachers and principals abused the children, and even the Haitian parents abused them too by beating them.

After the beating by the principal in the morning, my teacher gave us two homework assignments for the next day and I did one but the other one was too difficult for me, I couldn't figure it out; it was around ten at night and I went to bed as usual. The next morning after all, I got to school on time since my sister and I woke up earlier. My teacher was collecting the assignments and I asked her with respect if she could help me with the one that gave me a hard time last night.

She responded that that was my responsibility and that it was too late." Louisket où sont tes devoirs, a demandé ma nouvelle maitresse"? ("Louisket, where are your assignments?") I answered in French that I did one, but the other one was too hard. Usually she had a belt in the classroom to restore discipline. She came to me with her belt and started hitting me with that belt all over of my body and I was yelling. The other teachers came to see what happened, but didn't say anything. My father sent me a nice watch from the United States and it got hit by the belt and finally, I fell down and the watch crystal was crushed and my skin became red.

The minister of the private religious school was there, he heard me yelling, the principal was there along with other teachers, but no one told to my teacher to stop hitting me with the belt. I grew up in a country where teachers, assistant principals, principals, superintendents, religious leaders and the dictator Jean Claude (Baby Doc) Duvalier's regime believed that it was good for a child to get a beating anytime he made a little bit mistakes. There is evidences of significant levels of children abuse in Haiti at the time. Meanwhile the authorities felt the right to do so. The dictator Jean Claude (Baby Doc) Duvalier's vision was widespread in Haiti and hundreds tolerated the killing and torturing of opponents. Nobody could have spoken out against human rights abuses at the time, he would have lost his life, but it was clear that many Haitian people lost their good conscience in their own country.

My teacher was supposed to teach me how to do an assignment, and how to treat people with dignity, and to have a professional relationship with me. Instead of doing that she beat me and made me afraid of her, which gave me a lot of stress. It was clear that I had a bad day in my school. The same day I got beaten twice after falling down on the roads and the last one was harder. It was time for a change in Haiti.

When I got home, I didn't have time to tell my mother what happened. She asked me where my watch was and I couldn't answer her, I felt the pain all over my body. I answered my mother by crying many tears; the words couldn't come out. She knew there was something wrong and she was very impatient to have me explain what happened. Finally, my sister explained to her what happened. When my mother took off my clothes, she cried too because the skin on my back was red. However, in La Gonave if a patient became sick he needed to treat himself since there was no nurse who could have given him first aid. There was one doctor for every 35,000 Haitians and most doctors lived in Port-au-Prince, the capital of Haiti.

My mother boiled a little bit of water and washed me, especially my back. I couldn't take care of the animals that day and I had nightmares. I stayed in the house for a week and my mother accompanied me back to school the next week. She met with the minister and explained how I was being hit with a belt by my teacher. Anxious, my mother got upset and tears came out in front of the minister. She said that my teacher might not know the sorrow when a woman gave birth to a child. She had the right to beat me, but not as severly as my mother saw on my skin. The minister understood her and told her that would never happen anymore in his religious school.

The Haitian children didn't have a voice, but my mother defended me. But we still had no protection by law. Every child had to be punished when he made a mistake, with hide or belt, etc. As a result a lot of children preferred to stay in their house instead of going to school because they were afraid of their teachers.

There were so many factors to dissuade a child from attending any school in Haiti at the time. Economic reasons were major factors. More than 80 percent of rural Haitians lived below the poverty line. Even breakfast was a challenge for those children. 75 percent of schools were private, and only 25 percent were public which, was insufficient for 6 million people at the time. Most parents couldn't afford a private school for their children. For example, I had an adolescent cousin named Eveline Petion. Her father was my uncle. She was among fifteen children who went to school from Fregate to Zetwa in Lagonave. We were best friends since we were the same age, growing up in the same neighborhood, and we both enjoyed theater. My cousin Eveline was then living with my grandparents because my uncle was separated from her mother. My uncle Montilus Petion went to Guadeloupe, a French island and Lived illegally there. He couldn't go to work, stayed in the house and was unable to send money to take care of his daughter.

One day, Eveline was walking on the road and suddenly she dropped to the ground and didn't breathe a word. I called her several times, I whispered to her and I saw her mouth was tight and nobody could have opened it. The other children and I started crying out and we didn't know what to do. Eveline had been unconscious for more than fifteen minutes and we thought she was dead. When my cousin woke up she told us that she didn't have time to prepare her breakfast; she spent the entire day without eating anything, and she was dreaming about food. It was a heavy experience for me that day and we escorted her until she arrived home.

In Haiti, the women had to cook every day with charcoal and that made it very difficult for my cousin to cook each morning before going to school. Indeed, we didn't have a school lunch program. If our parents couldn't feed us before leaving the house we lost energy in the afternoon, and we learn less during our classes since we were walking two miles in order to attend the school. Sometimes when it was raining during rainy season, we just got wet with all of our supplies. We didn't fully prepare for it, but we didn't understand that at the time. Eveline was unable to continue her studies. Unfortunately, she died shortly after I left Haiti to pursue a new life in the United States. I didn't have a chance to see my cousin that I loved so much before burying her. I hope that her soul lies in peace.

Haiti is the poorest country in the Western Hemisphere. There was a high unemployment and the average annual income was under $ 400 at the time, and even this was falling because of high inflation. According to non government organization statistics, life expectancy in Haiti is 47 years for men, and 51 years for women. Therefore each time a young father died he would leave behind children in misery since he was the provider. As a result those children lived on the streets and became ill behaved in the Haitian society, not solid citizens.

Some children believed that when they went to school, it seemed like they just wasted their time. They could have made a lot of money by working on the plantations or cutting trees to sell because for cooking charcoal. Indeed, most children were hungry and there was little available work to do, except wood in La Gonave was in constant demand to make charcoal. That was why most of the children dropped out of school and went to work for land owners in order to survive. If some parents weren't demanding at the time, their children wouldn't go to school because it was a sacrifice to walk every day in order to have an education.

Most of the peasants knew that cutting the trees without replanting them was bad business, but the lack of motivation and education and because they were starving, they didn't have any other alternative. It was an economic misery problem which made basic education difficult for poor Haitian children. In other words, the biggest problems in my country were, and still are, socio-economic and educational.

While growing up, I saw many children who used to come to my parents' house just for food. Since my father was in the United States; they thought that my mom had a lot of money. Those children were called in French "rester avec"(staying with) but really meant "near slave." Their parents were among the Haitians who lived in poverty and were unable to feed these beautiful children. As adolescents, they needed to eat like everybody else, so they went from house to house, working as unpaid domestics in order to have a meal. In the countryside there was no running water on the property, so the main job for those children was walking for about three miles in order to get water. They carried a big drum full of water on their head at the age of six, seven, eight, nine years old etc. Since their parents didn't have anything, these formed out children were treated badly and had no respect from anyone. Even the Haitian community as a whole didn't see them positively. They had less affection than those whose parents were more fortunate. However, at the age of fifteen, all *"rester avec"* could have decided to leave and work for a salary since the Haitian law allowed them to get paid at 15. Those who came to my mother's house to work and received a home-schooling education while helping my mother. Sometimes, they needed food, not education and stopped studying.

When my father received a cassette from my mother explaining to him that I got beaten by a teacher. My father who was now living in a country of laws got angry and said if he were in Haiti he would fight with that teacher. It took my father three months to answer my mother because of the difficulty of communication with no regular mail or telephone to communicate with a relative abroad.

My father told my mother in a cassette to rent a house for us in the small town of Anse-à-galets, La Gonave a few miles closer to a school in order for us not to walk or to avoid of abuse. My grand aunt was living in the town of Anse-à-galets and suggested that my sister and I move to her house since she was alone. She gave us a room and then she cooked for us before leaving the house when we first got to her house. Now I was very excited to live in a small town, it was a great achievement and I didn't have to wake up early to move the animals. I loved the animals, but I would rather have just a dog and cat because I could feed them without waking up early every morning. My cat would sleep with me, while my dog had a little room to sleep. Finally, I was able to wake up at seven in the morning and walk just five minutes to school. I made new friends again like Philostin Jean Joseph who currently lives in Washington DC. I became his best friend when a teacher again wanted to hit me with a belt. He stood up and said to the teacher that I was not to be touched. He was older than me and although I came from the country, he was born and raised in the small town. Everybody knew my friend Jojo in town since he was from a famous family where his brother-in-law Louis Pierre-Louis was the inspector of the national education on the island. That day I was sitting next to him in order to avoid beating. Oh Lord, again and again some students were bleeding from severe beating before my eyes when they answered a sentence incorrectly or for not doing their homework. And because of my friend Jojo, the teacher never beat me again.

My great aunt had changed things completely for us, especially for me who loved going out with my friends. I was not a countrykid anymore; there was electricity in the town for about six hours from six p.m. to midnight while in my previous area I had none. I went out and came back around eight and my great aunt got angry and left my door open. There were a religious groups in Haiti who practiced voodoo and some of them worked at night especially after midnight when there was no light. A few of them were working as traditional with doctors and it was a way to make a living in Haiti. If someone got sick and those people knew what to do in order to treat him without going to the hospital. When the door of our room was open, my sister and I heard those voodoo groups outside and got panicked. We asked our great aunt to give us a key and she didn't answer us. Sometimes the door opened by itself.

When we woke up it seemed someone wanted to enter in the house around two in the morning. I called my sister to close the door and she was afraid to do so. Both of us ended up crying in fear. This was my aun't form of punishment-more effective than beating.

Most Sunday evenings, we left our village to go to the small town for week days and returned home each Friday for the weekends. We couldn't wait to finish the whole week to go back to our village and tell our mother what fear we went through in our great aunt's house. After school on Friday my sister and I arranged our lug gages and went back home. Later we explained to our mother how our great aunt treated us unfairly. At first my mother didn't say anything. But later I heard "c'est assez" (that's meant "is enough.") She sent my father a letter, but I didn't know what she said to him. After the end of the school year my mom told me that she bought her own house in the town and I was so glad to hear this news. My father and mother had both worked so hard in the village and continued in the same manner when he went to the United States.

It was a blessing for me and my sister. When school opened, we moved to our new house in town for the first time. My mother paid someone to take care of us and sometimes she stopped by. We were very fortunate to live in a magnificent house, luxurious, spacious, and furnished in good style for the first time. I didn't need to use candles to study anymore, since the house had electricity for about six hours every evening. I sat quite close to my brother, Jony and sister Kettelie, and helped them with their homework, which made them very smart in math, since we all lived together in the main town of La Gonave and left my mother alone in the village.

I became a "father image" in the house because nobody told me what to do and I had to decide now for my younger brother and sister when they had to study and prepare their assignments. My memory told me that all the problems had happened to me for a good reason. Since I shared a room with my younger brother, we could play music anytime we wanted without being bothered by anybody. Life was great while living in the town as a young boy. My father always sent clothes from the United States for all of us when he found someone going to Haiti.

I remember one Friday evening before I turned 10 years old. I returned to my mother's house in the countryside by myself. Then I met up with three brothers who never attended school because their parents worked for under $1 a day and education was very expensive in Haiti, so their parents were unable to send them to school. Two of the three boys I met that day were a little bit older than me. We knew each other since we lived in the same neighborhood. The one who was younger than me wanted to fight with me, but I was afraid since his two brothers were with him. In less than one minute, the boys told me that I had to give them my shoes and walk in my bare feet to go home. I didn't agree with them and they started beating me. I knew for a fact that I couldn't have fought with three brothers. It was a bad day for me and I cried out. They beat me on the ears, the top of the head, and my eyes. Finally, I was bleeding all over my face from a severe beating and I thought that I lost my teeth. After a few minutes of beating, someone came to ask the boys to stop beating me and they ran away. It was too late; I felt pain all over my body for a long period of time while there was no hospital in the countryside. As a result, I was unable to go back to school and stayed with my mother in the countryside until I felt much better. It was my last experience in Lagonave.

Suddenly, my father got an alien card and he was able to return to Haiti after a few years living in the United States. He returned to Haiti in order to spend time with us. We all were so glad to thank him for the great accomplishment of buying a house in La Gonave for us so we were able to attend school without difficulty. "wap fè plis pou mwen Louisket, se pa vrè?" responded my father meaning "you will do better for me Louisket, won't you?" I said yes to my father, that I will help him when I become an adult.

My sister Ifrancia sat next to my father, my younger brother Jony in front of my mother, but my sister Kettelie didn't want to eat her rice, sauce beans and beef. She stayed outside of the house playing with a little girl named Rosemonde who lived next door, and I sat next to my mother since my father was a stranger to me, but in his eyes. It seemed that he was having a good time with us. He had spent most of his time with my mother when he first got to the house. Nobody else could see him, but a few days later he gave us his time, played and talked to us. We had a good conversation with him. He said that he didn't have parents and he was working for us. Since I was very intelligent, he wanted me to have an education in the Capital of Haiti.

I was very excited about the idea, but my mother didn't agree petty reasons. She said that Port-au-Prince, the Capital of Haiti always had security issues. There were strikes. She was scared about the idea. My mother was the boss in the house and she didn't fool with me. When she said something she meant it. I asked myself why was she like that? In the Capital there were better teachers than in La Gonave and I would be able to explore the diverse neighborhoods while earning an education there. "I am worried," my mother added, after my sister said that she would rather stay in La Gonave than move to the Capital. We finished eating without a decision and my sister Ifrancia cleaned the table and went out as usual. To this day I feel annoyed that I had to live on the island of La Gonave, not the Capital. When it was time for my father to go back to the United States, he went to Port-au-Prince with me and he talked to my Uncle Ugin, who used to live with my mother after my aunts wanted to fight with her.

My Uncle got married in Lagonave and moved to Port-au-Prince with his wife. Then, my father gave my uncle money to look for a good school for me and took his address in order to keep in touch. With help from my uncle, I was able to start attending school in the Capital. My school was terribly overcrowded with teachers who had too many children in each class, but I was very motivated because I didn't want to disappoint my dad. In the end, I was among the best students who were very respectful, and talented in Spring Hill College.

Less than a year after I moved to Port-au-Prince, President Prosper Avril, a former colonel, a member of the National Council of Haitian government was overthrown in a coup d'état by General Herard Abraham. There were strikes all over Haiti and no one from the village could have reached the Haitian Capital.

My mother took a sailboat to visit me in Port-of-Prince and had to go the opposite way until law and order reigned. As a result of the coup d'état, many people lost their lives before President Avril resigned and was forced into exile as well, after his departure.

My mother was right when she didn't want me to leave Lagonave, but still I liked the Capital of Haiti better than the island because of the standard of living. Even in the Capital, a house telephone was a luxury at the time, but I was able to communicate with my father more often since there were some Telecoms, centers of communication, in each neighborhood. There was running water in my house and my life was better off. I only had to walk about fifteen minutes to attend school, and I enjoyed walking this walk. My aunt cooked most of the time and my uncle sometimes. Every morning, my uncle gave me money to go to school. Sometimes he fell asleep in the morning and before I left the house, I woke him up to shake his hands and made sure he gave me money in order for me to buy something in my school when I had a free period. He was a great uncle who I was going to miss later. Unfortunately, most Haitians saw their futures out of Haiti. My uncle was one of them who traveled to Nassau, Bahamas and he left me behind with his wife.

Then the absence of my uncle changed everything. His wife stopped cooking every day and I went to school sometimes without breakfast. By the time I called my father to send me money, I suffered a lot, but I didn't want to explain that to my mother because she might make me return to La Gonave. However, my dear cousin Eveline came to the house for a week and she had a bad experience. When she got back to La Gonave she told my mother what happened while she was there.

One day after my cousin left my aunt's house, my mother appeared at her house. When I came back from school and I saw her in the house. She cooked for me and of course I was so happy to enjoy her short visit for a little bit. She went outside with me and tried to interview me. "Louisket, tell me the truth," said my mother, I kept quiet and she added, "I am here for you" and "I don't want you to suffer". "Talk to me my son," and she continued: "everything has been concentrated on the Capital and the rest of the country is neglected as a result every youth hates the countryside". My mother concluded, "even if you don't want to tell me the truth, you gonna have your desire." By the way, the same day my mother talked to my auntie-in-law about renting an apartment for me, since my sister would move and live in Port-au-Prince. Tomorrow afternoon, we started searching for an apartment. We found a real estate agent who gave us all the information about renting and helped us find a bedroom apartment, but not in a great condition. It was obvious that apartment rental in the capital was not so difficult at the time. My mother and I did everything in just one afternoon. The landlord agreed to sign the lease only if I wouldn't let anybody occupy my room for longer than a week, and no pets or animals were allowed in my room. Finally, upon three times notice, the landlord might revoke the lease. I agreed with all of that and signed the lease for a year. My mother paid for the whole year and we went to buy some furniture for the apartment. On the day after we paid the lease, we moved in and my mother talked to our new neighbors about helping me in case of emergency. Most of my neighbors were students who came from different places such as Tomazeau, Aux Cayes, etc. and they told my mother that we could study together.

I was a teenager who absolutely needed the support of my parents. However, I came from a family who valued education although they were struggling with many children. Life was not easy for my parents. Both of them were working very hard for all of us while suffering at the same time since they could not see each other on a daily basis.

My mother left me and hoped that my sister would move to stay with me, but she didn't like the big city. She felt uncomfortable with it and each time she came, she spent a week or two and returned to the island. After my mother left me by myself, I was thinking about one thing. If she came back and asked me for my report card, what would I tell her? I committed myself to not make any mistakes in order for me to encourage her let me be and achieve my goals.

Overthrow Aristide Regime

While I was in the capital, a progressive priest named Aristide Jean Bertrand, who was expelled from his Salesian congregation, became the first democratically elected president in Haiti, after almost two hundred years of independence from France. President Aristide lost his father when he was a child. A Salesian priest helped him receive a good education in a Catholic School in Cap-Haitian, the second Capital of Haiti. After high School, President Aristide crossed the border of the island of Hispaniola to study in the Dominican Republic and became a Salesian priest in 1983 after many years of studies in Haiti and abroad.

Father Aristide had been one of the greatest opponents of Jean Claude (Baby Doc) Duvalier and many members of Duvalier's regime didn't like him because they thought his speech would drive people to liberate Haiti from a dictatorship, so they and tried to kill him several times. On September 1991, shortly after becoming president, Aristide was overthrown by a military coup d'état, which killed thousand of Haitians and forced him into exile in Venezuela and in the Unites States. Now the army took power and killed civilians especially in the Haitian Capital. Many parents in Haiti were afraid to send their children to Port-au-Prince. I had to spend three months back on the small island of La Gonave. When I returned to the house, I met a Christian counselor named Arnold Balde. He was a Catholic missionary who came from Hinche, Plateau Central. He lived in front of my parents' house along with three Brothers.

Brother Arnold helped me as a youth deal with some issues in my life. I was allowed to participate in different seminars. Furthermore, I saw him as an answer from God since I didn't have a father in the house who could have given me good advice. I kept in touch with him and he always talked to me about Jesus and President Aristide. He compared their lives as two human beings who loved the poor and were persecuted because of that. In addition, Brother Arnold read the Bible and analyzed the different passages step by step with me. Finally, I became his best friend and I learned a lot from him. It had been a dream of my life to have such a good teacher who was patient and answered my questions. I always had questions for Brother Arnold. Why he left his area to come to Lagonave? How he got there? Why he couldn't have children as a Brother?

He answered all my questions and I started attending the conferences with the four brothers who were living in a four bedroom house. I drove all brothers from one city to another when they had conferences. Many people now knew me on the island. I saw now the obligation to receive baptism or christening after my conversations and interactions with other religious groups. I prayed with the Catholic missionaries three times a day and they handled my questions with extraordinary love. Suddenly, I became a member of the Catholic Church.

My own experience with those missionaries as a youth inspired me to become priest. Therefore, Brother Arnold referred me to a French congregation where I met later Father Pierre Lebeller, a French priest specialized in counseling and helping young Haitian teenagers become priests. Every month I had a conference with Father Lebeller along with more than forty young boys. All of us wanted to be priests. We sang and prayed each time we met. Father Lebeller taught us the life of Jesus Christ and encouraged us to love the poor. He said as students we needed to look for information about other countries in order to know the world. I enjoyed meeting the other youths every month and listened to Father Lebeller. He gave me a scholarship so I could I attend the French alliance in Haiti for a year.

First Trip to the Dominican Republic and the history of the island of Hispaniola

After High School, I traveled for the first time to the Dominican Republic to learn a different culture, and especially to understand the treatment of Haitian workers who were enslaved on sugar plantations in the eastern part of the island. When I was in eleventh grade my history teacher gave us several lectures about the Dominican Republic, and I was very excited about visiting this neighbor country first and to relive its history. Haiti and Dominican Republic share the same island of Hispaniola, but have very different cultures.

At the end of the fifteen century Christopher Columbus, an Italian, navigator, colonizer, and an explorer for Spain left Europe traveling west to find another way to several Caribbean islands, which named "West Indies." Then, Hispaniola was one island with about 4,000,000 Amerindians who had been living there for more than 5,000 years in the Caribbean (according to the *New World Encyclopedia)*. Before the Europeans discovered the island on December

5, 1492, Haiti and the Dominican Republic used to have multiple names such as Ayiti, Bohio, or Kiskeya under the Arakan people. However, the Europeans considered the whole island as the colonial headquarters for the Spanish exploration and before returning to Spain they enslaved the Amerindians. According to many historians, the Europeans brought some diseases to the island and as a result most of the Amerindians died while the colonizers were seeking gold and slaves to help them exploit the lands.

Since many of the Amerindians died by enslavement, massacre, and diseases, at the beginning of sixteenth century the first enslaved Africans arrived on the island under European masters, and less than two decades later slaves were brought directly from Africa and established all over the entire island of Hispaniola. That is to say Haitians and Dominicans both were slaves under Spanish powers; both were working very hard on the plantations in order to serve the Europeans have their wealth at the time.

The power of Spanish colonials was not limited to the island of Hispaniola. They went all over the American continent from West Indian colonies, south and north and conquered and enslaved the Native Americans who owned the lands. At the end of the seventeenth century, most of the Spanish colonizers moved to Mexico to seek new wealth and agreed to give France the western part of the island of Hispaniola that is called today "Haiti," while they continued exploiting Dominican Republic, the eastern part of the island.

Haiti was Born with Tears

Under France as a new colonizer, Haiti became one of the most important plantation economies in the new world with the Africans slaves who worked the sugar, coffee, tobacco, rice, and cotton on the plantations in the morning, in the afternoon, and in the evening, without a break for about three hundred years under both Spanish and French control. In July 4, 1776 the American people made history as the first nation to declare its independence in the Western Hemisphere by saying to England "enough was enough," and won independence in a great battle between British and American soldiers. But it was not the end, in October 9, 1779 more than five hundred Haitians fought under the French flag for America against British forces in Savannah, Georgia. It was one of the bloodiest battles and as a result many Haitians lost their lives for this great country.

I believe that the American people needed our support in the difficult time in order to win its independence and the three rights that the founding Fathers considered to be natural and unalienable: "life, liberty, and the pursuit of happiness."

After the complete victory of American independence, there was a Haitian soldier named Henri Christophe among those Haitians fighters who returned from the thirteen colonies to Haiti. The African slaves continued working seven days a week on the plantations, and their beautiful children were abused by some colonizers, and they did not have any right to say anything. Some of them ran away from the plantations. There was a statute in Haiti called in Haitian Creole "Neg Mawon" or "Marron inconnu" meant "the unknown slave in order words

Commemorating those who ran from the plantations towards the forest before the American independence." The French revolution in 1789 shook up the entire France empire, and two years later, thousand of the Haitian slaves cried out and fought to make history as the second independent country in the Western Hemisphere, and the first black Republic in the new world. There was a Jamaican born named Boukman, a slave, voodoo priest who was one of the instructors of the slaves at the time. Most of the slaves liked him and listened to him when he asked them to do something. Boukman used the African religion to free the island. He led a ceremony, was deep in the mountains, in August 14, 1791 with only one goal to overthrow French rule in Haiti. He made the slaves believe if they died during the battle they would wake up in Africa. Over the next few days, the slaves' army controlled the countryside and destroyed most of the plantations. However, the conflict between Blacks, Mulattos, and French white made the war very difficult to win and little bit longer. A great man named Toussaint Louverture, another remarkable leader of the African slaves after Boukman, joined the battle. He was a self-educated former slave, and Haitian Patriot who worked very hard to overthrow British and Spanish forces and free Haiti. Toussaint Louverture became a commander in-chief of the colony appointed by Napoleon Bonaparte, the French Emperor.

He tried to unite Black, Mulatto, and French colonizers. That is to say under Toussaint Louverture regime racial discrimination was not an issue in the island. He encouraged the white French owners to return to Haiti and the former slaves to work for them, but this time would pay the former slaves. Most of the mulattoes and former slaves didn't like the idea at the time and organized an insurrection against him. When Toussaint did not know what to do in difficult time for Haiti, he called for help from our great neighbor, the United States of America.

One day President John Adams, the first vice president for two terms, and the second president of the United States was asked by General Toussaint to support him against his rivals in Haiti and he received a significant amount of aid from President Adams which helped him defeated those extremists. Later Toussaint wrote the first constitution which ensured liberty and equality for all peoples regardless of race or color in the colony. But he named himself a "governor for life," which made the emperor of France upset and he sent 20,000 French soldiers under the command of General Leclerc to defeat the vision of Governor Toussaint Louverture. After a long battle between the two forces, Governor Toussaint agreed to meet with General Leclerc to sign a peace treaty, which would allow the former slaves to continue enjoying their freedom peacefully. It was a trap and Governor Toussaint got arrested and was transported to Fort de Jour, France on a waiting ship. Before leaving the island, Toussaint said, "In overthrowing me, you have cut down in Saint-Domingue only the trunk of the tree of liberty. It will spring up again by roots, for they are numerous."

He never came back. According to Straker, D. Auguste the Haitian hero died in Fort de Jour on April 7, 1803 by apoplexy, pneumonia, and starvation. The French prison was very cold. Toussaint lost his life for the good cause of freedom.

After reading the account of Governor Toussaint, I was thinking about a leader alive today, the former president of South Africa, Nelson Mandela, who loves the diversity of his country, and encourages the black South Africans to work together with the white South Africans despite all his years in prison. Likewise, Toussaint Louverture did not want to fight with the European colonial powers. He disliked the division and injustice. He fought all his life for freedom and equality, not only for the African slaves on the island, but also for every nation in the world because he loved peace.

After the death of Toussaint, slavery was re-implemented by France. It seemed Toussaint lost his life for nothing. But under his regime the island knew a little bit of freedom. The slaves were united again and fought against French colonizers. Emperor Napoleon was dealing with many different battles especially in Europe. After losing some of his soldiers on the island, he accepted the former slaves as a nation. France later sold its territory, Louisiana, for a much needed money to the United States of America because Napoleon was afraid that what happened in Haiti might happen in Louisiana, which was a border of the early United States. Furthermore, France made Haiti pay 150 million gold francs for its independence, money the island did not have, but did not have a choice, so it struggled many decades in order to pay this debt.

Above all, Haiti became a source of freedom. It was the first new world government to abolish slavery. Many leaders left their countries to visit Haiti in order to better understand how to free their countries. Simon Bolivar was one of them. Was received by the first president of the island, Alexandre Petion, who gave him all materials necessary in order to free the Latin American countries. Bolivar left Haiti on April 10, 1816, went to Venezuela, but failed to win a battle and returned to Haiti once again. This brave general was resupplied by President Petion and created the first Venezuelan flag near Jacmel in the south of Haiti after studying Haitian history for more than two months in Haiti. When Bolivar got back to his country, this time, he won the battles, and became one of the greatest South American generals who liberated a country.

Simon Bolivar did an excellent job by liberating his South American country. One of our Haitian leaders, Petion, would contribute to successful revolutions through other South American countries. That is to say Haiti has had a rich history and culture. Haitians used to be proud to live in their own country. They had enough food to feed them and didn't have to look for a better life abroad when Haitians occupied the whole island for about twenty two years.

I took a small plane to go to the Dominican Republic and when I arrived at Las Americas International Airport, near Santo Domingo, the Capital of the Dominican Republic, I asked myself what was wrong with Haitian leaders? It was obvious to me immediately that in terms of infrastructure the Dominican Republic made more significant progress than my country. I was very happy for every Dominican. I was met by the secretary of a former Haitian diplomat in the Dominican Republic, Edwin Paraison. He picked me up from the airport and dropped me off in a good place where Ambassador Edwin had a Dominican friend who gave me food three times a day. I spent the first night and when I woke up in the morning, Ambassador Edwin sent a Haitian student to where I was staying and was told to show me around the Capital of the Dominican Republic. This student came from the Haitian elite who attended la Universidad Autonoma de Santo Domingo (The Autonomous University of Santo Domingo). He was fluent in French, Haitian Creole, and Spanish. He visited his school with me and introduced me to his classmates. After three hours of exploring the Capital, we stopped by a restaurant to have dinner. Later we visited the Haitian Embassy, which was located a few miles from where we ate. I met the secretary again who welcomed me in his office. We talked about the differences between Haiti and the Dominican Republic. How Raphael Trujillo killed about 35, 000 Haitians in a few days, 35,000 Haitians went there not to fight with the Dominicans, but only because their leaders kept trying to kill each other and there was unstable politics which made Haiti very weak. These Haitians thought that they could have found a better life next door instead they were getting killed. Furthermore, the secretary emphasized the importance of visiting Dominican Republic as a young man. He told me, the future of Haiti was in your hands, guys. The Haitian student and I left shortly after the little conference with the secretary. I wondered why about 35,000 Haitians got killed, and I asked my fellow Haitian to take me to Bateyes. He told me that I had to be careful since Bateyes was a devil place to visit especially for Haitians. I might get hurt by Dominicans if I went there. The Haitian student gave me some advice, he knew the Capital City of the Dominican Republic very well since he had been living there for more than three years, and I tried to follow his advice. "This is not Haiti," said the student," where you can do whatever you want to do", "this is a foreign country, and you need to bring your passport with you each time you plan to go out". Instead of going to Bateyes, the student took me to Boca Chica, one of the most beautiful places where the Dominican elite lived or went on vacation. It was a fascinating place and took a lot time to truly explore the modern shops, clubs, casinos, restaurants and hotels with antique charm. We met a Haitian man who had been living in the Dominican Republic for about ten years and he gave us a good lecture about some under-class Haitians workers who constantly crossed the border to reach the Dominican soil and lived illegally while working without a salary for some Dominicans owners. For example, poor illegal Haitians cut the sugar cane while most of the Dominicans did not cut cane. He said that those Haitians resided as sugar cane workers in Bateyes and did not have any accessible healthcare, or clean water, or education and they remained undocumented. This guy was very intelligent and he spoke Spanish fluently. I was shocked as a young man, and the more he talked to us the more I wondered what he was going to say next. I had a lot of questions for him and I invited him to have dinner with us. I can still see the face of this great patriot, who took the time to teach me and the other student what was happening to our sisters and brothers who left our country because of poverty, violence and unemployment. The Haitian student had chosen a nice restaurant, which was located on the south coast of Santo Domingo. I had seen many people in the area, and I was very curious and excited to learn a different culture. There was a beautiful Dominican woman who came to welcome us and asked us to sit down. I remember that I sat in the middle between the student and the Haitian immigrant. The first one was on my left and the second one on my right. The server placed a water glass in front of each of us. A few minutes after we had entered there were many people at the restaurant, and we found three menus on the table. The Haitian student ordered some rice and chicken, and I can't remember what kind of meal the Haitian immigrant had chosen. After looking at the menu, I decided not to eat because I was very sad. While the Haitian immigrant and student were eating, I was thinking about life in a foreign country. It was the first time I had left my country, and I did not know anything about life abroad especially in a country, which shared the same land with Haiti but was so different. I had thought everything was the same.

The Haitian immigrant told us that Haitians and Haitian-Dominicans are not accepted as Dominicans because they characterized by the colour of their skin. Many Haitians descendents who were born and raised in the Dominican Republic could not go to school because they did not have identification papers especially if their parents lived illegally there. Those children were neither Haitians nor Dominicans even though they spoke two different languages: Haitian standard Creole and Spanish. He told us how he got to the Dominican Republic. He paid to cross the border and the Dominican military at the border did not care about what he was going to do in their country. Both Haitians finished eating and I paid for them. Therefore, it was time to say au revoir, meant "good bye." We hugged each other after learning about the misery of the Haitian immigrants in the Dominican Republic. I wanted to ask the guy one last question before finally we would leave each other, but I was afraid to ask him. I did ask if Haitians had been humiliated in the *Dominican Republic* why had they not decided to return to their own country. He answered me what about those who were born Haitians-Dominicans but undocumented? The Haitian constitution did not recognize them. What they were going to do over there since the Haitian government did not do anything to relieve the poor, and they were also mistreated by their own government. All I was saying was that the situation was out of control, and I was sure it was going to explode. If they could have done something about it in advance, it would save some lives. I was getting tired and frustrated. I only wanted to get rested that evening.

At the time, I was very young and did not know anything about life abroad. The following day, I attended a mass at the **Cathedral Primada de America** in Santo Domingo, everything was in Spanish. It was a beautiful Cathedral, which had Gothic architecture and sculpture. I believed the cathedral was among the most popular buildings in the entire Dominican Republic. According to the Haitian student, thousands of visitors attended the Cathedral each year because it was a place of pilgrimage with lovely decorating. Evidence of the Spanish colonial power and the influence of Haiti in Dominican history offered me a broad experience in a few days. I relived what I learned from my Haitian history teacher when I was in 11th and 12th grades, and I perceived that this rich heritage was preserved in such good order that it made the **Dominican Republic** a fascinating place to visit.

It was time for me to return to Haiti, and I wanted to thank to Ambassador Edwin Paraison for being nice to me and paying all fees to make me have a wonderful time in the Dominican Republic. But he was on vacation; I never had a chance to see him face to face. I did not know Ambassador Edwin Paraison by name until my advisor, brother Arnold Balde gave me his number and sent him a letter in order to welcome me when I visited the Dominican Republic. I learned later that Mr. Edwin Paraison was an Episcopal priest who worked with the poor in the Dominican Republic, and had become consul to **Barahona** while helping the Haitian workers who were dealing with injustice in the plantations. I also thanked the Haitian student who never left me behind and dedicated his time to help me have such a good time for the first time in a foreign country. Finally, the secretary of the Haitian ambassador took me back to las Americas International Airport and I took the same airplane to return to my country after a wonderful new experience.

Now I had a lot to tell my family and friends. All of them were very excited to know what happened on my first trip. I had to explain several times when my friends stopped by just to say hello. I had a lot of friends since I was a captain of a soccer team. I used to organize different sports activities every summer in La Gonave. I told everyone that Haitians needed to wake up otherwise the Dominican Republic would be our future. The saddest part of this was that Haitians occupied this country for more than two centuries, while the people there were getting richer than us. I added that our leaders had to avoid corruption, in order to ensure a good future. That reminded me that the well-being of a nation depended on the education of its rulers. In just one week away from Haiti I saw a lot of things that the Haitian leaders needed to do. The social structure needed to be discussed. The Haitian leaders were certainly not saints, but I had more expectations for my country. I was tired of hearing of violence in Haiti, tired of child abuse in school. I planned not to go back to the Dominican Republic, but to Caracas, Venezuela. In less than three months after returning to Haiti, I traveled to Venezuela to get information about universities.

I met a priest named Andre in Carapita, Antimano. He was born and raised in Belgium, French speaking country, which shared some of the same culture as Haiti. I talked to him about Father Pierre Lebeller and Brother Arnold Balde, who had accompanied me while I was in high school. He asked me for a letter of recommendation and I called Brother Balde and he sent the letter to me. While I was in Caracas, I worked with a Haitian group who attended Father Andre's Church and I went to Centro Venezuela y Americano *(CVA)* and learned Spanish. But I kept thinking about the poor Haitians who were living under poverty and really needed someone who cared about them. My old friends stopped attending schools because their parents could not afford it and they went to cut trees in the forests. They believed in me and always thought one day I would become something, since my father was in the United States and I would be able to help them. I felt like I had some responsibility towards those unfortunate Haitians. It was not about me now, whether I stayed in Venezuela or returned to Haiti, my future was ensured because my parents cared about all of us and spent their money for us. Indeed my mom moved to the Haitian capital in order to take care of us and she built a house while living there.

Traveling to the Dominican Republic and Venezuela helped me grow up a little bit faster, and gave me new ideas about serving the people. As a young man, I was hopeful that I could make a difference on our little island. When my friends did not hear from me, they said that there was a tree in the foreign countries, and anyone who went under that tree would forget their friends. I discussed my concern with Father André and he told me that I had to continue with my studies first, and he explained to me how he became a priest. He did not know what to do with his life after spending a year in the army, but he was born and raised in a Catholic family and he received a call from God and he followed Him.

After what happened to me when I was youth, I did not want a new generation to continue with the old system. I followed my call to work for the Haitian people. I returned to Haiti after a while and attended University of Toussaint Louverture. I chose Political Science because I felt the pain of the Haitian people. I did not want to live my whole life seeing Haitian children dropp out of school because their parents were unable to pay for them. I was not better than them, but only the universe knew why I got some education and privilege and my fellow citizens did not.

While attending the University of Toussaint Louverture, I had the opportunity to open a health center in Drouillard, about two miles from the Capital City of Haiti. I called it "Louisket Pharmacy Center." Brother Balde Arnold and my parents supported me highly. I had five professionals who were working for me: one doctor, one nurse, two certified nursing assistants and one house keeper. I bought medicine from Caracas, Venezuela for my Pharmacy and as result we treated many people in Drouillard. But the doctor told the patients that the Health Center belonged to him. He got jealous maybe because a lot of people came for treatment in the center. When I learned of his opinion, I talked to him about it. The doctor left me and later opened his own office next to me. However, I wanted to serve the Haitian people, not to fight for personal gain. The doctor was a fellow Haitian above of all. I sold the center to a well-known man named Fritzner Boyer, who had a Night Club in La Gonave. His cousin Marie Edithe Dazy was working with me as a nurse assistant and wanted to buy all the items.

I felt not doing anything was not an option, since I had to provide for my fellow Haitians the way my parents provided for me. Therefore I decided to open a **Multiple Business Services** to help the Haitian people. I traveled to meet the Haitians who lived in Guadeloupe, Martinique, Saint-Martin, Curacao, etc. Most of the time, I traveled through Dominican Republic in order to reach French speaking countries. I took a ship from Sainte Lucia to go to those islands. I made a lot of friends going there. Each time I met the Haitians, they sent money to their relatives in Haiti. It was not easy to find someone who went back and forth and they paid me for the service. I kept in touch with them and traveled more often to help them.

Running for Representative to the Haitian Congress

When I was a senior at the University of Toussaint Louverture, I decided to run for Representative to Congress. I had helped *Fritzner Saint-Fleur* get elected as a Representative in the previous election, but he decided not to run again. I wanted to run because I kept thinking about my childhood-how I got beaten by teachers and could not say anything. Indeed, I had traveled outside of Haiti and had experienced how other governments treated their own people. I saw a huge of emergency for Haiti ; and I wanted to be a Representative to the Haitian Congress, in order to make changes for which the island was in desperate need.

My travel experience and my childhood have highly influenced me to make a sacrifice for a new Haiti. I knew that I might lose my life, since politics in Haiti is very dangerous and dirty. However, I was so proud of my ancestors, who fought hard to give us freedom that I was unsatisfied with their successors who did not do anything to help those who were starving. I felt like the Haitian leaders made worse decisions for Haiti than any other leaders of independent countries. This was not what I wanted for my country, and I was ready to pay any price for my homeland. There could be enough wealth in the island for every Haitian to live well. Things could get better, if really, we had control of our own destiny.

I studied Haitian history and wondered what happened after independence. I found that we did not do well as the second nation in the Western Hemisphere. Our violence and corruption made most of the people very poor. It is a shame for all of us, but not all of us were corrupted. My great, great, great, great, great grandparents in colonial times worked seven days a week, twelve or fourteen hours a day. They did not have rights, and they lived shorter lives, since were abused or sent to prison for little mistakes. Our founding father tried to correct the injustice and he was right. He was proud to fight despite of all the difficulties he endured to free the island, but he couldn't prevent us fighting against each other. According to Haitian history from 1804 to 1999 there were about 22 presidents who were overthrown, three were assassinated, seven died in office and many caused big problem.

I believe democracy is the best condition for development of a country. Therefore when there is a coup d'état, the people who take over are not democratically elected, and the term democracy becomes absurd since their power was not earned but taken injustly. Too many Haitians lost their lives, too many Haitians still cry, so it was time for me to try to end all of that. Unfortunately change isn't easy.

What happens on the island when a government is overthrow?

Each time there is a coup, the men, women, children (mostly civilian) get killed by the brutality of the military. For example when one president is overthrown at least 10.000 Haitian civilians lose their lives since. We had about 22 coup d'états from 1806 to 1999, in less than 200 years of independence. As a candidate for representative in 1999, I told people: multiply 22 coups d'états x 10,000 dead = 220,000 Haitians who got killed by their own leaders, not by disease, old age or Spanish or French colonizers. I believe land becomes an evil place when Haitians do not give the Creator the power and follow his commandments. We lost so many lives on the island of Hispaniola. Haitians have been crying since Columbus discovered the island. Not all of us like violence, not all of us like coups d'état, not all of us like selling drugs to destroy other people, and not all of us like fighting against each other. But we have let our leaders get away with it all.

When I have seen these kinds of bad governments, I always thought our first step should be education for every Haitian. We could be a great nation if we had peace of mind and stopped mistreating our citizens, especially our children. I believe it is not too late. There is enough land on this beautiful island for every Haitian to live happily without depending on the Dominicans or other nations.

I think we should forgive our former leaders for all of their sins and let them return to Haiti and return the money they stole from the nation.

If we really want a new Haiti, we should show the world that we love peace, not violence, and we are committed to live with each other on the island of Hispaniola. We must not let our fellow citizens humiliate us for whatever reason, and nor accuse other nations before we fix our own.

Let me be explicit, nobody can pay me to hurt my family. When a police officer enters into a house where there is domestic violence there is a reason.

The police are needed. When we have foreigners on the island of Hispaniola each time we fight against each other, each time we abused our fellow citizens, it is because we have shown we can't run our own country. When there is no peace in a family, when there is no leadership, authority must rein in order. Peace comes with education and education opens our eyes, and makes us understand the world. We should stop the injustice toward one another which made our country weak for many decades. We ourselves have destabilized the economy, and forced thousands of Haitians look for a better life abroad. So many people lost their lives trying to escape Haiti. Families suffer when the fathers live away from them.

I also believe Thomas Jefferson, who said that, "people get the government they deserve." Unfortunately, in Haiti the reality of this statement is tragic.

Why did we overthrow a president who was elected by its citizens? Why do we make thousands of fellow Haitians cry all the time on the island and abroad? Why do we abuse our children? Why do we accept corrupt leaders? Why do we expect other countries to help us if we do not help ourselves?

It is a shame now to talk about an island which had such potential as the second independent country in the Western Hemisphere. It is a shame for all of us who built a negative image of our country at home and abroad, and nobody is happy about it.

It is enough. I no longer want to see the Haitian children stay on the streets without going to school. I did not live and die to see 80% of 9 million Haitians live on poverty. I no longer want to see Haitians killing each other. I no longer want to see my sisters and brothers unable to get an identification card because of their skin colour in the Dominican Republic. So I stood up on behalf of the people of La Gonave to fix this mess, and I was ready to pay whatever the price for my unfortunate Haitian constituents.

As a young man, I accepted the call to run as a Representative to Haitian Congress in May 20, 2000 because I believed that I was different from the traditional Haitian politicians. I had a good heart and experience abroad, which my fellow Haitians needed. I saw how the other nations treated their citizens. I did a lot of research about the United States, France, and Canada and found that they have had stability in their politics because they did not fight against each other. Their former presidents had term limits. Gave up the leadership jobs every 4-8 years, and stayed in their countries, to advise the young ones only when asked. I was very excited about having the same system in my country in order to progress. I thought one of the best ways to achieve change was to be a member of the state government. We were five young Haitians who wanted to represent our La Gonave in the Haitian Congress: Me, Gilvert Angervil, Marie Ganette Galliotte, Daniel Bertrand, and Fritzner Eliassaint. I was younger than the other four candidates but had more experiences abroad than they. A Haitian must be at least 25 years old to run as a representative, must be a registered voter, a Haitian citizen at least four years prior to the date of election, and must have a letter of criminal record. I had all the documentation that the president of the provisional Electoral Council required. I agreed with Damour Nadal, the coordinator of the political party, Tet Ansanm, to represent his party in the Haitian Congress. Gilvert Angervil represented Lavalas Party; Marie Ganette Galiotte represented Lespas de Concertation, Daniel Bertrand Mochrena, and Friztner Eliassaint represented Louvri Barye.

I did not see my opponents as my enemies, but rather real citizens who wanted to make a change in their country. I gave some credit to them since they also saw the necessity to fix the system we had at the time. I campaigned to the entire La Gonave Island to talk about freedom, abuse against children, human rights. I said to the La Gonavians that I was running to end the beating of our children in every school system in Haiti; I did not want to see or hear of any child touched by a teacher. I was running to help build the economy where owner/ farmers and the plantation workers will have the support of the Haitian government. We absolutely needed financial reforms in Haiti after many years of economic crisis. As a representative I pledged to make sure that the government controls the money and spreads it out fairly, by making extending a modern infrastructure to all areas outside of the capital. I wanted to help La Gonave to become one of the best departments in Haiti where tourists could come to enjoy our beaches.

But I said "I won't be able to do that if you don't vote for me." Our economy sank into a great depression after we won our freedom, and we needed people like Toussaint Louverture in the Haitian congress to vote for good laws which would help the Haitian markets function fairly. We needed commonsense rules in Haiti because our ministers were not following such rules on their own. Education, housing, health care, clean water, employment all were challenges in our country even for professionals who spent a lifetime to receive education. Electricity was a challenge and construction was a mess in the entire country. Where were our ministers, I asked my supporters? It was enough and we had to change. My supporters saw me as a mediator who could have helped them relieve the problem, and they were ready to vote for me.

Everywhere I campaigned, I told the people that as a representative, I would fight to ensure that our children, who wanted to have a formal education, would be able to do so. This was why I was running as a representative for the Haitian congress. I gave speeches in different small towns and I kept repeating that I was not running for representative to criticize anybody, but to move ahead. We were too behind, and we must stand up and walk on our own with our neighbors. I was running because some Haitian politicians did not have honest hearts, did not know how to lead, did not follow the promised our ancestors, especially Toussaint Louverture. They slept too much, did too little, and made our country weak while they accused other nations. We should respect ourselves first, our citizens first, and the rest of the world would then respect us and give us back what we worked very hard to earn.

I told my audiences that I felt the Haitian authorities made bad decisions for our country. With me we could stop the violence, instability, and coups d'état. With me we could show the world that we were a good nation. Indeed, I saw the world as a mixed family whether someone is Mulatoe, African-American, African, Haitian, White, Asian, but functioned together regardless of race. I opened my heart to live and discuss the future of the island with everyone whether they like me or not. We overcome those childish things like hate, violence, mistrust.

I hate violence and when I see people are suffering, I ask several questions: Why we are here in this little world? What is the definition of life? What is next? Where are we going after life? When are we going? How can we learn to care about each other?

And before leaving this world, I would like to see one thing for my people to receive a good modern "education." If we used our heads, we would stop hating each other, our neighborhoods would have peace, and we would not need police officers in our neighborhoods, and people would trust us.

I announced my campaign for representative at Sainte Bernadette, a Catholic School in La Gonave; I saw so many supporters there. I was introduced by Mesguerre Julien, a mayoral candidate in the Tet Ansanm Political Party, who is now a Judge in La Gonave. It was a new day in my life with the cheers of my supporters. I thought that I already won the title "Député" Representative. I was looking forward to being a public servant and to help to form a perfect union in our little island. My advisor, Balde Arnold, who returned to Plateau Central several years earlier, stopped by and endorsed me. It was one of the best endorsements I ever had. Another advisor, Jean Lochard Jean François, also endorsed me. I was blessed to have such citizens, who were highly respected in the La Gonave community, endorse my candidacy for Representative to the Haitian Congress.

What did I accomplish as a young man in Haiti?

In my speeches, I always explained to my supporters that I saw the world differently from the way my opponents did, and I told them what I accomplished before becoming a candidate for Representative.

As a young man, I opened a Health Center and a Pharmacy to treat Haitians who got sick in Drouillard, and multiple business services serve the Haitian people who were in desperate need of care. As a Representative, I would continue to fight for those who were crying for food, clean water, healthcare, education, and so on. I would fight as well for our diaspora the Haitians who lived abroad and had taken a foreign nationality, but they still supported the Haitians who lived in Haiti. In order words, the diaspora contributed in the development of Haiti. By preventing the Haitians living abroad and their children from serving Haiti, I believed wasn't right. As a Representative, I would work hard with other Representatives to amend the articles on dual nationality in the Haitian Constitution. In the 21st century, fellow countrymen who had dual nationality, for one reason or another ought to be able, to return to Haiti and serve their country. All Haitians who were born outside of Haiti including those in the Dominican Republic who had been crying for decades for Haitian birth certificates, would be able to have their recognition as our citizens.

In my point of view, our politicians were afraid of our diaspora for decades. What if truly educated people really wanted to return and get involved in the politics of their country? During the summer 1999, I traveled to Guadeloupe and I met some fellow countrymen who lived in Pointe-à-Pitre, Magallard Gosier, Sainte-Anne, and Trois-rivière. Some of them wanted to return to Haiti. One Sunday afternoon, my cousin Dalice Joffrey, took me to a party, which more than one hundred Haitians attended. They asked me if I were elected what would I do as Representative, since they had dual nationality (Haitian-French) and were dreaming about returning to their native country. They all were professionals. I answered the question by telling them that I did not like their exclusion from our political process, and as a Representative I would adopt the same position. By the way, we would realize this dream only through a constitutional amendment, if and only if your family members and friends voted for me. Indeed, I was personally convinced that Haitians who lived abroad should not only have the right to run for public office, but also should vote by absentee ballot where they were living. Despite the difficulties we faced in the island, it was not impossible to unite our fellow Haitians who were looking for a better life outside of our country. There was no doubt about the Haitian diaspora who contributed to the economy of Haiti with hard cash. According to the Inter-American Development Bank recently Haitian expatriates sent about 1.87 billion US to their relatives who lived in poverty in Haiti. Therefore I was right to support a change to the Haitian constitution which would give rights to the Haitian-Americans, Haitian-French, Haitian-Dominicans, Haitian-Bahamans, Haitian-Venezuelans, etc. to serve their country at all levels.

Furthermore, when I returned to my native land, I spent over a year advocating for our people who lived abroad; for homeless families that I met before I ran for public life. Those people could not eat and if they got sick they were unable to see a doctor since there was no hospital in the village. As a young man, I had tried to eliminate a major obstacle to moving those people out of sickness. I opened my heart and used my money, knowledge, time, as well as my energy, to care about those under-represented populations in my homeland.

I was running for Representative to the Haitian congress for a reason. When I campaigned in Lagonave, I heard so many sad stories. I met many Haitians who never had a pay check in their life; they did not make any money at all. Consequently no one could have talked to them about universal healthcare. It would be an audacity of hope.

That was the way life was and remains today in Haiti. I did not think there should be a moment of celebration in my country while the majority of these people were starving. In terms of education, most of the children stayed on the streets, since 75% of Haitian schools were private and only 25% public which made education expensive in Haiti. Those who made 1 U.S. dollar a day were unable to send their children to school. I felt that some children would never be able to realize their dreams or show their full talents unless I took action. I could not tolerate the misery in my country.

I was delighted about the potential improvements for my country. I was against beating the students and abusing the children who were called" ***Restavek***" used as "slaves" all over the country.

I thought I could help since this country needed new ideas to end corruption and improved government accountability. I thought I was going to help promote foreign investment, stability, love and solidarity among Haitians. I admired my fellow Haitians so much and I was inspired by those who gave freedom to this island, which had been unstable for more than 200 years. I felt that Haitian politicians lacked idea. I entered the race as a middle class man who was hopeful and had a clear vision to help my people get out of poverty.

As a candidate for Representative to the Haitian Congress, I was excited about what could happen between the Dominican Republic and Haiti. I did research about the Haitian massacre in the Dominican Republic on October 1937 under Rafael Trujillo where more than 35,000 Haitians got killed by Dominican soldiers and civilians in a few days. I said to myself, from 1937 to 1999, more than sixty years, our fellow countrymen lost their lives in the Dominican Republic and we haven't taken a day of memorial for them. I felt like we were a nation of bad faith, while some did have good hearts, since most of us abroad sent money to our relatives in Haiti. When they called us we could not sleep knowing their pantries were empty. I said to myself it was not one Haitian who got killed, it was not two, but 35,000, a genocidal massacre like this hurt. My fellow Haitian deserved a day where every Haitian would

Remember their fellow citizens who died in the Dominican Republic. The young Haitians and Dominicans would learn about the history of both countries. As a representative I was planning to work with others in order to include a memorial day for these unfortunate Haitians in the calendar of Haiti. I wasn't scared at all even though I was unhappy with the Haitian system political.

As a young man, I put my hat in the race to continue the dream of our founding fathers, who fought for every Haitian to live in peace. As a representative I would convince my colleagues to take a day off in the memory of those fellow Haitians. Indeed, I believed that children born in a foreign country who had Haitian parents deserved the right to choose Haitian or dual nationality. I would propose new laws which would allow those undocumented Haitians, who were born in the Dominican Republic for instance, to have social status as Haitian citizens because they were my countrymen by blood. It was too much for those unfortunate people who had been discriminate against for so long in Dominican Republic.

It is a very sad situation that Haitians who were born and raised in the Dominican Republic could not have a birth certificate, and when they had a problem, nobody could represent them. For instance, a person without a birth certificate is unable to work in a regular factory since he is illegal, and cannot travel either. But I had faith that God was with my nation in the good as well as in the bad years.

Do I like Dominicans?

Not all Dominican agreed with the bad treatment of Haitian workers in their country. Thanks to God who gives strength to Dominican religious groups (including the Catholic Church and evangelical Christian churches, the Civil rights groups and inter-American court of human rights) who have been defending the rights of illegal immigrants in the Dominican Republic. They want the Dominican government to reform the law so that Haitians born in the Dominican Republic would have the same rights as those born of Dominican parents. Therefore, I answer yes, that I do like most Dominicans. I believe by showing them love perhaps they will have compassion for my fellow Haitians who have been living in their country. Indeed, whether we like it or not Dominicans are feeding almost one million Haitians, and we have to pray for them as a nation who shares their wealth with us.

On the other hand, I certainly believe that the Haitian leaders should do something to unite their citizens living not only in the Dominican Republic but around the world. Indeed we especially need our great neighbors, the United States, Canada, Brazil and, the rest of the world to overcome the misery in

Haiti. We have to read about history, but not make people pay today for what a previous generation did badly.

Nevertheless, during my campaign for representative to the Haitian Congress, I went to the masses to get their support in order to make the changes I was dreaming about. I hoped in the end, that the voices of the Haitian people would be louder than that of the traditional politicians.

I was ready to work night and day to take care of those who had Haitian blood in the Dominican Republic or outside of Haiti, and 80% of those unfortunates who lived in Haiti through a constitutional amendment, education, healthcare, and our development programs. I delivered many speeches to my supporters. There was no question that compared to my other opponents, I would win May 21, 2000 election without fraud, since the people who endorsed me opened their hearts and minds to elect me as a Representative to the Haitian Congress.

The more I read about Toussaint Louverture, the more I loved peace, because he had chosen union over division in order to preserve the freedom of the island and for a while made the Haitian institutions function. Then, I saw myself as a mediator. I could have spent my lifetime trying to convince my fellow Haitians that we needed to be united. I felt again and again that I understood better what happened the 80% of Haitians who were starving than the other traditional politicians. That is to say that I felt I was situated to help Haiti move into new era.

LEGISLATIVE AND MUNICIPAL ELECTIONS ON MAY 21, 2000

About 4,245,384 registered electors were called to vote for their candidates by Leon Manus, the provisional Electoral Council (CEP), but due to violence the election had been postponed several times. On March 19 and April 30, 2000, while the term of the National Assembly had expired, there was neither representative nor senator in the Haitian parliament. The president of Haiti at the time governed by decree, which was not good at all for a democratic country. The Haitian people needed to elect 19 senators, 82 representatives, 133 municipal boards and 564 boards of administration of communinal sections at time.

Many members of opposition parties had been persecuted by the supporters of the Lavalas party. As a result, ten had been killed by fellow Haitians, who later burned down the headquarters of the United Democratic Convention. That meant all candidates spent lots of money to campaign each time the president of Provisional Electoral Council fixed a date, which date was never respected. I was one of the candidates who were inspired by the 35th president of the United States, John Fitzgerald "Jack" Kennedy who stated, "ask not what your country can do for you, but what you can do for your country," and was ready to fight for every Haitian in order to do something for my country.

I was running for Representative to Haitian Congress when ten Haitians got killed, not by foreigners, but by their fellow Haitians for power. I felt sad when I saw the Politicians who should be an example for their supporters. But they did not say anything about the violence against children, against women, and against journalists. I felt that we were lost and we did not have any idea how to develop the island, which the founding father risked his life for a country where every Haitian should have a normal life, not a freedom to hate our fellow Haitians. Usually I am afraid of blood and I respect life, however, I said to my supporters that we needed a new revolution in Haiti, but not with guns. It should not be violent, but a revolution of new ideas that the 21st century required. It was an exciting campaign and many polls in my district revealed that I led. By the way, the Organization of American States (OAS) had sent more than 200 international observers, and finally on May 21, 2000, thousands of electors turned out to elect nineteen senators, 82 representatives, 133 municipal boards and 564 boards of administrations of Communal sections (CASECS).

Only the Lavalas candidates had access to voting booths even though four other candidates for representative, including me, called the president of our political parties to identify the problem we faced in the island with the Lavalas candidates. They did their best to support us, but nobody could have stopped the Haitian authorities from using their power unjustly against us. The international observers denounced the fraud that we had received from CEP members They were afraid of certifying the final results due to so much fraud in the elections.

It was true that the president of the *Provisional Electoral Council* (CEP) had been escorted by some diplomats across the border of the Dominican Republic in order to escape persecution. He reached American soil and later sent a letter to Mr. Edgard Leblanc, who was the president of the Haitian Senate at the time. Mr. Léon Manus said in his letter that analysis of the legislative and local elections of May 21 showed that it is not legally valid for many reasons:" Massive electoral fraud, incorrect and illegal method of counting the votes disregard for laws governing runoff elections." Furthermore, he continued to say that the police, charged with maintaining order and public safety, unfortunately participated in a number of fraudulent acts. As a result the parliament arising from this process is illegal, illegitimate, and built on false premises, and couldn't be validated per confidence in civic and patriotic honor.

Even though the results were contested, the Haitian authorities did not do anything to help the opposition leaders and ensure stability that every Haitian needed. This hurt the entire country several years later, with the persistence of the opposition leaders.

I did not agree with the opposition leaders who tried to block all Haiti by striking all the time even if the leader of the Lavalas party finally agreed to give up some seats. The way I thought about it, everybody was out for their own interest. Instead of fighting against each other, the opposition leaders should have worked harder to show the Haitian people that they cared about them and let the country run peacefully. One of my opponents was my best friend and I did not see her as an enemy. We both wanted to change the economic misery in our country and work for the Haitian people. Not too long ago I called her several times when I heard that one of her sisters died in a collapsed house in Haiti.

Final Goodbye to Haiti

My father had been living in the U.S. for decades and he filed a form I-130 in Florida for the four of us to join him. As a resident alien my father had the right to apply for his relatives to immigrate, including his wife. The application of my father was approved and several years later my mother along with sister Judette and brother Stanley received a temporary evidence of lawful, admission for permanent residence in the United States of America. My sister, Ifrancia, and younger brother, Jony already lived in Fort de France, Martinique. I felt alone in the island without my family members who were seeking a better life abroad. A few months after losing the election, I received a letter from the U.S. Embassy in Haiti, and I hired Mrs. Sainte-Ange who had been working for the Citadelle Agency. She spoke English fluently and was able to assist me with all necessary documentation to immegrate. She also offered me a wealth of information and support as a visitor and resident alien to the United States of America. A few months later, I got a temporary evidence of lawful, admission for permanent residence to U.S. Most of my supporters were aware that I was about to leave Haiti, and some of them wanted me to stay and run again in four years.

I didn't have the heart to leave my country for life and leave behind my family members and friends. I was very sad and depressed, but I had to leave everyone in the island for while within one month of receiving the authorization. My parents kept calling me from U.S. and worried me that I would lose my green card if I continued staying in Haiti. I hadn't had a chance to say good-bye to my grandparents who lived in the countryside and was unable to communicate with them because of no phone or mail. But I sent my cousin, Benissoit, to tell them that I was leaving and if they wanted me to bring something from them for my parents I would. My grandparents received the news and were expecting me to stop by and to say good-bye any way. But I did not go for several reasons. As a former candidate for Representative to the Haitian Congress, I got popular and the peasants always thought that I would bring something each time they saw me. When I didn't have money to share with them, I just remained in the Haitian Capital. Another reason was, I knew myself and I had self doubt that I would be able to survive in an English speaking country and start all over again as an adult. I asked the following questions: Did I really want to live abroad? How I was going to do that? Why? Was I going to leave my fans? I had doubts in living in the United States of America because of the different culture. I saw myself in Canada or France. But several months later after I arrived, I fell in love with this country and I felt like I wasted my youth and potential in Haiti.

Finally, I bought my ticket on American Airlines and on June 2, 2001 I decided to enter the United States of America. Before I left my parents' house, I closed my eyes and prayed to the Lord for giving me birth in a country where most of the people were starving, but never ignoring them, and opening a door for me for a new life in a powerful country. I asked Him not only to protect me where I was going to live in the United States, but also to help me stay away from bad people. I could not count how many Haitians, who came to the United States, and instead of going to school for a better life, wasted their lives on the streets, sold drugs, got deported. I didn't want that to happen to me. One of my sister's friends took me to Toussaint Louverture International Airport. "Mwen pakonnen kilè nap wè anko" ("I don't know when we'll see each other again,") my sister's friend said. I answered him that it depended on fate, and there was a silence for a while until I got out of his car and shook his hands and thanked him for helping me.

Inside of the airport there was a long line to check my luggage, but I was certain now that I would live the American dream. I met a passenger who came from Lagonave and lived not too far from my parents' house in Florida. I was very excited to meet her since I wanted to surprise my parents because I did not tell them that I would definitely come. I was waiting in the line to check my luggage while talking to the Haitian woman. It was my turn now to check my luggage and enter to the Immigration. It was around eleven a.m. they announced the American flight and I got on the airplane. There was a stewardess who guided me to my seat with a good welcome to American Airlines. I became an alien in one hour and thirty minute flight from Haitian to Miami, Florida. The passenger who lived near my parents's house and I shared a taxi. My family was so happy to see me. "Pou kisa ou fè sa?" ("why did I do that?") said my mother.

She called our family members and friends that Louisket finally made it to the U.S. My parents' house became full like a Church with Haitians who came to greet me, but not to cry out this time rather to enjoy the investment that my parents had made more than a decade ago. Some of them talked to me about the election; they thought I was going to win it. I talked a lot that day and I needed to rest. But I spent only nine days there. I was home sick. On June 11, 2001 I bought a ticket and returned to my homeland. I met my Uncle Ugin in

Fort-Lauderdale and he took me to Miami International Airport. My parents got upset with me because I didn't want to live the American dream. My father told me that the United States of America was the world's capital and "you could have done a lot if you stayed here." "I don't like Haiti for you Louisket," concluded my father.

I understood where my father came from, but I didn't like the neighborhood they were living in. I saw so many children on the streets smoking and the way they dressed made me question my future. Also, I went to learn English two days after I got here, and the teacher began with A.B.C. I felt like it was too much for me, a man who got popular and very advanced for my country. Why should I have to start all over again? I got frustrated in trying to learn English and chose to return to Haiti right away. I was totally wrong.

My parents understood and let me go, but never stopped telling me that my future was in the United States. Now I began thinking about how my country was my destiny. Although I tried to make a change but because of some Politicians in power who did not believe in elections, my dream did not come through. I believed peace came through strength, and the Haitian people had to keep God in the forefront to get out of poverty. I had forgiven those who stole the legislative elections May 21, 2000, because I did not like to fight with my fellow Haitians, and I was not ready to be a stranger in the United States.

Finally, I decided to live the American dream in a moment when the world was crying because of the loss of love ones the September 11, 2001 terrorist attacks. It was very tragic, not only for America, but the rest of the world. The President of the United States, Georges W. Bush adopted new policy, and announced that the United States would make preemptive strikes to avoid another terrorist attack.

At the time, I felt hurt for several reasons. On the one hand, I was born and raised in a Haiti which stole opportunity from me. On the other hand, the United States of America had opened a door for me and allowed me to live the American dream, while other people, not being well intentioned, attacked its citizens and killed thousands of them.

On October 7, 2001 thousands of men and women in the U.S. Army, Marine Corps, Navy, Air Force, and Coast Guard stood up to defend this powerful country. They said to everyone who lived in the United States of America "Don't cry, don't cry," and "don't surrender to pain". They stood up to let us know that our tears were precious for them because they believed in freedom, justice, and peace. As a result they went to Afghanistan with coalition forces to destroy the whole organization of Al-Qaida, which used Afghan territory as a base of operations for terrorist activities.

On October 21, 2001, less than three weeks after the departure of U.S. troops to Afghanistan, I decided to move to and remain in this powerful country. It was a very difficult transition for me. I was thinking about the Haitian heroes who fought for freedom on the island, but I was unable to enjoy it, because the Haitian leaders moved the entire country backward. I never stopped talking about Toussaint Louverture; I was one of the candidates for Representatives to the Haitian Congress who praised Toussaint Louverture. He was the man who stood up to tyranny on the island of Hispaniola and changed course of the island, even if he went too far by naming himself leader for life. Even though I was no longer living in Haiti, I still would have liked to have seen a new direction for Haiti in the 21st century.

Before I left Haiti I wrote a poem for the people who lived in the island of Hispaniola and later it was translated to Creole, Spanish, and English at Temple University in Philadelphia, Pennsylvania.

"A black life is cheap in the island of Hispaniola"

Why is there black, black, black?
Black like the shadows, ows, ows
Black like night, night, night
Why fighting against each other in the little Haiti or around the world, world, world?
Why beating our children in Haitian schools, schools, schools?
Why can't Haitians born in the Dominican Republic cannot have a birth certificate, certificate, certificate?
Why is there black, black, black?
It's the same question we ask today, today, today.
Why is n't the world a family, mily, mily?
But it's a sign of hope, hope, hope
That the world, world, world
Says no, no, no beating for all children, children, children
Stop fighting against each other, other, other
Yes, to a birth certificate for all without exclusion, exclusion, exclusion
Yes, to freedom for every nation, nation, and nation
No, to discrimination, tion, tion
Fortunately the United States, Canada, France, Brazil, Spain, welcome new people, no
matter what race, color, age, origin, origin, origin
And this is why the world needs our prayers for peace, peace, peace

There was a lot happening in my country while I was growing up, and trust me, as a young man I went through a lot before moving to the United States. I had tried to adjust to life's transitions, and I felt frustrated many times I wanted to return to my country because I was a person who was fortunate to have many friends in Haiti, especially after the legislative campaign which made me meet so many great people in Haiti.

Now I was ready to do anything for an education in order to have a normal life. My brothers-in-law who took the sailing boat in 1991, after former president Aristide was overthrown, now lived in Tampa, Florida. He and others advised me to move there and I thought I was going to grow socially and intellectually since they had been living for about a decade in the United States before I got here. They told me there was no way a black man could complete a college degree in this country. I disagreed with them because I learned in high school in Haiti that Martin Luther King, Jr had more than one degree, I learned about Jesse Jackson, Sr, a political figure, clergyman, civil rights leader in the United States and candidate for U.S. president, and other black leaders who were highly educated like pastor Al Sharpton in Brooklyn New York. I had been inspired by these leaders and was determined to pursue my goals of completing a degree in the United States. I told my brothers-in-law that I believed if the American authorities allowed us to be here, there was no doubt they would like to help us succeed and to behave well in their country. There was no way I would have a good standard of living if I did not go back to school in America, and I certainly believed a professor would evaluate me based on my intelligence, not because of my skin color. There were some Haitian folks accusing people of discrimination without evidence. If my parents were rich, I would have been able to stay in Haiti or Florida, not travel a lot. But I needed to look for a better life now for myself, since my parents did all they could to bring me to this great country, which had many opportunities. I loved my brothers-in-law, but they had wasted their time in the USA by not setting more schooling, and thinking that American teachers were not fair with Haitian or black students. I left them with tears in my eyes in Florida, and moved to Long Island, New York. It was an emotional goodbye because we wanted to live together. I was unsatisfied with them and their lives.

Hungry for an Education in the U.S.A

I traveled to New York because I was looking for a place to live forever. However the cost of living was so high in New York that I moved to Philadelphia, Pennsylvania where I spent almost a decade.

My parents were always there for me, I had enough money to survive, but I was hungry for education. I got frustrated when I went shopping and was unable to describe what I was looking for. I met so many people who wanted to communicate with me; but I couldn't say the words and I just smiled because of my lack of English. I thought one of the best ways to fix this problem was to go back to school and learn the English language, which would enable me to experience the American dream. Now I had only one dream to learn English and math to become a civil engineer in the United States. I attended the Community College of Philadelphia enrolling in the liberal arts program. But I did not have enough money to enroll full-time. When I was in high school in Haiti, I liked math, physics, and chemistry a lot. Therefore, even though I did not speak English, I could understand the numbers. I started with one math course and I got an A.

On November 22nd 2002, I went to bed around 11:00pm and the weather was fine. When I woke up the next morning I saw a white landscape for the first time in my life. I wondered what happened, and I called my best friend John in New York. He told me that it was snow. I was born and raised in a tropical country, with little exposure to other climates. This meant I had ever seen snow before. Therefore I didn't recognize it and I felt even more alien in the United States of America. But I had watched TV in Haiti and saw snow on TV so I knew what it was. I don't have to explain how difficult it was for me to drive in snow. I rushed quickly to the balcony to take pictures and went outside to experience snow for the first time.

This is me in wintertime

The following semester, I met with an advisor named Mrs. Louise. She asked me why I didn't register for more classes since I was a great student. I explained to her that I couldn't afford it because I just had a blue collar job which didn't pay enough. She was a beautiful white woman and spoke French fluently. *"Attendez-moi Louisket,"* (wait for me Louisket) responded Mrs. Louise.

I sat in her office and didn't say anything. Mrs. Louise kept trying to phone someone for about thirty minutes. Finally, she found the person she was looking for, but I didn't know what she was talking about spoke on the phone in English. After she hung up the phone, she told me in French that I had to go to the financial aid office, where someone was waiting for me. When I finished with the financial aid person, I should come back to her office. I followed her advice. Outside of the financial aid door, I saw a white man who called my name and I answered him. We entered his office and he asked me in English for my personal information and gave me a paper. But I didn't know what was going on. I brought the paper back to Mrs. Louise and she registered me as a full time at the Community College of Philadelphia with financial aid paying everything for me. That was the beginning of my American dream. This prove to me that Mrs. Louise didn't judge me according to my race. She emphasized that everyone has responsibilities to others and gave me an equal of opportunity to try to succeed. In order words, Mrs. Louise was an American who saw the value of investing in human potential.

Then, I came from the island of Hispaniola where education was expensive and despite violence and political instability, we believed that the future would be better than the past. I was very happy and committed myself to do well at the Community College of Philadelphia because I was free to pursue my personal goals. It was really hard for me before I got this help.

While I was at the Community College of Philadelphia, I heard that Haitian rebels took control of many cities in Haiti. As a result, hundreds of Haitian police officers and civilians got killed. The second term president Jean Bertrand Aristide failed to force the rebels to step down. He left the island at the end of February 2004 without his two beautiful daughters who were then in the United States of America. He is currently living in South Africa with his family, but dreams of returning to the island.

In my opinion, whether someone likes President Jean Bertrand Aristide or not, the Haitian people voted for him for five years and he should have been allowed to complete his term without being forced into exile. He was the only politician who showed love to the poor more than 80% of Haitians, and he inspired them. He should have remained in Haiti and invested in our country. For the first time, we had a powerful political party and a leader who helped many kids have an education, and opened the press both TV and radio for them. The coup d'état destroyed all of this.

My homeland has become weak again. Every coup d'état brings more destruction for the Haitian economy, more tears for the Haitians living in Haiti and abroad. Haiti can't continue moving from coup d'état to coup d'état. The founding father wanted us to enjoy freedom by choosing our own representatives, but not to use force against each other to get that representative.

After the coup d'état, Gérard Latortue, a former foreign minister of Haiti in 1988, became the prime Minister of Haiti on March 12, 2004. He persecuted the supporters of President Aristide, and most of them went to prison without seeing a judge for many months. Gérard Jean-Juste, a Roman Catholic priest, liberation theologian, and a spiritual leader of Haitian Americans was among the people who were beaten and arrested several times because he didn't agree with the interim government of Gérard Latortue who excluded the members of Fanmi Lavas Political Party.

Father Jean-Juste, a human rights activist was working hard to improve the life of poor Haitians and he helped many refugees flee persecution under the *Duvalier* regime. He had been living in Miami, Florida for many years and ran an organization there. He never stopped defending the poor and telling the truth anywhere he traveled because he believed in justice, democracy and unity. A Bishop named *Thomas Gumbleton* visited *Father Jean-Juste* after he returned to Haiti and was in the National Penitentiary. He said that Father Jean-Juste didn't have enough room to lie down and there was no light in his room. As a result, Father Jean-juste became ill with injuries from his beatings, but was denied medical treatment by the Haitian government, even when a US diplomat tried to help him with a physician. "They can take my body, but not my soul," said Father Jean-Juste. His treatment in my homeland hurts all of us whatever our belief.

I compare his life with that of Jesus. Both of them were persecuted because they loved the poor and justice for all, both of them got arrested for the same cause and were accused for something they did not do.

This Haitian priest who was educated in the United States died several months after he got out of prison. "Don't cry when I die," said Jean-Juste, but he left the rest of his cause for all of us to do. He died because he cared about his people. He wanted to make a change in his country and suffered a lot before leaving the world without accomplishing his ultimate goals. A prisoner of conscience under the Latortue 2004 regime, he fought against violence and felt injustice was an aberrant or sinful lifestyle. He believed that Haiti made history as the first black Republic for every Haitian live well, but our history was never meant to include putting our fellow citizens in prison without evidence, killing or beating them for no reason. Father Jean-Juste we loved you and we will never stop talking about your legacy.

Father Gerard Jean-Juste isn't the first priest who died for the poor in Haiti; Father Jean Marie Vinghcent and Pastor Sylvio Claude also lost their lives in similar conditions.

Picture of Father Gérard Jean-Juste

My homeland has become weak again. Every coup d'état brings more destruction for the Haitian economy, more tears for the Haitians living in Haiti and abroad. Haiti can't continue moving from coup d'état to coup d'état. The founding father wanted us to enjoy freedom by choosing our own representatives, but not to use force against each other to get that representative.

After the coup d'état, Gérard Latortue, a former foreign minister of Haiti in 1988, became the prime Minister of Haiti on March 12, 2004. He persecuted the supporters of President Aristide, and most of them went to prison without seeing a judge for many months. Gérard Jean-Juste, a Roman Catholic priest, liberation theologian, and a spiritual leader of Haitian Americans was among the people who were beaten and arrested several times because he didn't agree with the interim government of Gérard Latortue who excluded the members of Fanmi Lavas Political Party.

Father Jean-Juste, a human rights activist was working hard to improve the life of poor Haitians and he helped many refugees flee persecution under the *Duvalier* regime. He had been living in Miami, Florida for many years and ran an organization there. He never stopped defending the poor and telling the truth anywhere he traveled because he believed in justice, democracy and unity. A Bishop named *Thomas Gumbleton* visited *Father Jean-Juste* after he returned to Haiti and was in the National Penitentiary. He said that Father Jean-Juste didn't have enough room to lie down and there was no light in his room. As a result, Father Jean-juste became ill with injuries from his beatings, but was denied medical treatment by the Haitian government, even when a US diplomat tried to help him with a physician. "They can take my body, but not my soul," said Father Jean-Juste. His treatment in my homeland hurts all of us whatever our belief.

I compare his life with that of Jesus. Both of them were persecuted because they loved the poor and justice for all, both of them got arrested for the same cause and were accused for something they did not do.

This Haitian priest who was educated in the United States died several months after he got out of prison. "Don't cry when I die," said Jean-Juste, but he left the rest of his cause for all of us to do. He died because he cared about his people. He wanted to make a change in his country and suffered a lot before leaving the world without accomplishing his ultimate goals. A prisoner of conscience under the Latortue 2004 regime, he fought against violence and felt injustice was an aberrant or sinful lifestyle. He believed that Haiti made history as the first black Republic for every Haitian live well, but our history was never meant to include putting our fellow citizens in prison without evidence, killing or beating them for no reason. Father Jean-Juste we loved you and we will never stop talking about your legacy.

Father Gerard Jean-Juste isn't the first priest who died for the poor in Haiti; Father Jean Marie Vinghcent and Pastor Sylvio Claude also lost their lives in similar conditions.

Picture of Father Gérard Jean-Juste

When there is violence in my homeland, my prayers are with all those who suffer. I can't stop thinking about the poor who don't have a pay check. Believe it or not, that affected my studies. I kept looking for information on the internet while at the Community College of Philadelphia in Philadelphia.

I took more than forty credits at the Community College, while learning English, and transferred to Temple University in Philadelphia, as a math major. Now it was time to prove to myself that my advisor Mrs. Louise was right to give me this scholarship even if I didn't have any doubt.

Before transferring to Temple, I was living near Broad Street in Philadelphia. As a young man living by myself, one night I wanted to go to Church and pray to Jehovah God. I was living on the second floor and while leaving my apartment, two men with guns told me to put my hands up. I was afraid and obeyed them quickly. "Never mine this is not the guy we are looking for," said the gunmen. Finally they let me take the stairs to exit, but I felt unable to attend the service when I got outside. I came back to my bedroom apartment and went to bed. I felt unsafe now in my neighborhood. I had a nightmare and when I woke up in the morning, I talked to my landlord about what happened to me. I decided not to finish out the lease and he agreed with me. I moved to housing on campus since I didn't want to lose my life.

The first four days living on the Temple campus were horrible for me; I avoided several fights. I learned two years later from a Race and Religion Class at Temple University that the race I historically belonged to had carried some negative stereotypes as a group, which was bad in the eyes of the white world. This resulted in too many homes nowadays that were lacking a supportive, conducive and positive family structure, and children forced to raise themselves. On the other hand, I read about many positive examples, like Queen Latifah, a Grammy award winning rapper, actress, and activist who challenged and broke many of the steotypical views of black women involved and influenced by hip hop lyrics. In her 1993 hit "Unity" she focused on many of the issues that were affecting the African American Community, particularly the women. On the other hand, in Sister Souljah's book **The Coldest Winter Ever**, the main character winter was an example of a "ride or die chick," who by the conclusion of the book was imprisoned for drug possession and had the side of her face sliced during a fight by a "gangsta bitch." The ironic thing was that the drugs that were found were hidden in the teddy bear that her dope dealing boyfriend gave to her as a gift, and when he realized that she was being arrested he fled.

The negative stereotypes about people of color affected me as an alien student who was very motivated to have a formal education in the United States, but not to sell drugs, steal or fight with the American citizens.

One morning, while I was sleeping in my room, I heard a male voice who called my first name several times it was not the first time he did that since I moved on campus. I woke up and asked him what happened. "Louisket you have to leave the apartment today," said the guy. I didn't say anything because I was an alien in the United States and the guy was in his own country. I wondered if I should have stayed in Haiti, but my fellow Haitians were still fighting each other too. Look at the way the Haitian authority killed Aristide's supporters, put them in jail and excluded them because the power of Aristide on his supporters. When we don't have a peaceful society, we can't develop a country and most of citizens suffer. The lack of peace makes Haiti weak. That's another reason most Haitian youths and adults would prefer to look for a better life abroad.

Anyway, I committed myself not to fight with any American whether he was black, white, Latino, or Asian, and even if he / she tries to destroy my will power. Finally I looked at the man. He was a very attractive man who was taller and bigger than me. He felt he could yell at me, but I didn't answer him because he was totally wrong. He approached close to me, and I was afraid of fighting. I tried to get out silently and he raised his voice. "Louisket, Louisket, Louisket I am talking to you," said the guy. I kept quiet and said to myself that I wasn't at Temple University to fight. If the man gave me a chance to stay here in peace, I would achieve my personal goals by completing a degree in either math or civil engineer. While I was thinking I heard "No, no, no, you can't do that to Louisket, you can't do that to him, he is too nice," yelled many white students.

The guy said that he never lived with people with color before in his life. Therefore he asked me to leave the building. Finally, he got upset and wanted to beat me outside of the door. However, God sent some students to help me escape from the beating and they called the police. Here is the incident report for further information (Temple University # 05-14042).

When one person says no, a thousand others say yes. My experiences in both countries make this true. It is a true story, which occurred while I was looking for a better life. I didn't know what to do since I was doing the right thing going back to school as a legal alien in this great country. Finally the police officer came to my apartment, but the guy already left the building. "He is a crazy guy," said the officer after printing out his picture. Indeed, the officer wanted to kick him out of the building; nevertheless, I refused because I wasn't here to make the man feel uncomfortable in his own country, even though I knew very well about my civil rights. I left the building with tears in my eyes. Later changed my majors to French and Spanish for several reasons.

Prior to attending Temple University, as a student at Community College of Philadelphia, I was one of the students that stood out in the crowd at (CCP) because of my active involvement in student affairs. Since I would like to become a teacher, I decided to become a math, French, and Spanish tutor in the Learning Lab. I tutored 25 to 35 students each week, in-between my classes. My supervisor told me that I did a great job, I then decided that I would like to volunteer at Duckrey Elementary Public School in Philadelphia, after I became a student at Temple University.

I spent four hours every week and helped the American students do their assignments. Later I worked for the city of Camden Board of Education in Camden, New Jersey. Tutoring isn't easy if a teacher doesn't have patience. But I liked the children. When I met them on the streets, it was fun for them to call me by my first name since I have a funny name. Indeed, they always had a question for me about Haiti.

While I was a student at Temple University, I traveled to Mexico City, Mexico. I spent a week there before I took a bus to Oaxaca, southern Mexico with 23 American students, and a Spanish professor named Sylvia. I lived with a Mexican family for the whole summer. I Attended the Cultural Institute Oaxaca, Mexico which was located a few blocks from where I stayed with my host family. Every morning before I went to school, my Mexican hostess prepared breakfast for me, then I came back around noon for lunch and walked back to school again. I did that five days a week. Saturdays and Sundays, I dedicated my time to learn more about the history of Oaxaca, Mexico. There were a number of impressive discotheques and nightclubs, which were also part of Mexico's lifestyle. I was very interested in the history and culture. A few things are still vivid in my memory. For instance, the older architecture was very nice, Plaza de la Constitution, Palacio de Gobierno, and most importantly the religious architecture in Oaxaca. While I was in Oaxaca, I visited Mexico City, one of the largest cities in the world with 22 million inhabitants.

I met some international visitors who told me that they found in Mexico a diverse legacy of different pre Hispanic cultures. I never imagined that living the American dream would include a summer in Mexico to help me tell my story. I am very grateful for this experience.

As an exchange student, I helped the Mexican students to learn English as a Second Language (ESL) and I taught them French. By helping Community College students, elementary, high school students, and Mexican students formulate principles and morals; I potentially made a difference in their entire lives. I found that teaching others was extremely rewarding.

Besides my involvement in academics and leadership roles, I was very active in area Churches. I have always had a passion for the down trodden. One of my biggest dreams was to build a school in Haiti to educate those who were unable to receive an education in my motherland. Since I knew that I wanted to teach and travel throughout my life, I was trying to learn as many languages as possible. Haitian Creole and Standard French are both spoken in Haiti. I attended classes in Venezuela and Mexico where I learned Spanish. And I am learning English in the United States of America. So, I now speak four different languages. I wrote poems in the French department at Temple University in Creole, French, Spanish and English with Dr. Laura Spagnoli before completing two degrees in French and Spanish literature. I accepted a new position as a French and Spanish teacher in Miami Dade County in Miami, Florida. I left Philadelphia to move back to Florida. Most of my friends were so happy to see me after many years of studying in Pennsylvania.

When some of my friends heard that I became a teacher at North Miami Senior High school, they went back to school because they were inspired by me. I immediately became their advisor because my friends wanted to know what to do in order to complete a degree in the United States, and it was a pleasure for me to help them.

I taught four French and two Spanish classes Monday through Friday. I belonged to a great team in the foreign language department who were very helpful. I had a very good salary since I was teaching full-time. I liked my students even though some of them didn't listen well, and I became a mentor time for those who wanted and needed help. I felt very sad when I left North Miami Senior High School in Miami, Florida. An assistant principal named Salgado called me and he asked me to stay, but unhappy with one of the leaders who treated teachers and students unprofessionally. I decided to leave and looked for more education.

Later I accepted a teaching assistantship at the University of Maine in Orono. I drove from Florida to Washington DC with a beautiful girl named Louidnie and I spent a night with my best friend Philostin Jean Joseph. When I woke up, Jeanclaude, and Fervil gave me a tour of the White House before going to Philadelphia, for a week and then spent two weeks in Montreal, Quebec, Canada.

Some of my friends and family thought I wouldn't be able to survive in Maine since I grew up in Haiti and make up less than one 1 percent people of color of the entire population in Maine. I remembered Father Pierre Lebeller, a French priest who taught me when I was a teenager in the Capital of Haiti that we needed to be proud of ourselves even if we were too fat, too skinny, too short, too tall, too black, too white, too brown, or too yellow, etc. Therefore, I didn't want to limit myself to live anywhere, and I always thought positively even if sometimes I was disappointed. That's life, isn't that true?

Finally, I drove for about seven hours from Montreal, Canada to Portland, the largest City in Maine. I stayed on campus with many Americans while attending the University Of Southern Maine Portland, Maine. I took one graduate French course and two education courses. I was the only black person in my class in Portland, Maine. My professors treated me more than fairly and I made so many good friends in Portland in a short period of time. It was quite an experience to remember. Then I moved to the University of Maine in Orono, in order to begin classes in the fall semester. Orono is located about two hours from Portland, Maine. I met a quiet hero named Sandy Lyons in Orono, Maine. She was the secretary of Modern Languages and Classics at the University of Maine. She lived by herself and wanted to rent a room in her house with someone. She accepted me as a tenant until I completed my masters degree in teaching French at the University of Maine. She was so nice and respectful. She cooked for me and left a note on the table if I was sleeping in.

I had my own room and I shared the washroom, kitchen with her. She was nice to me all the time. I realized that getting to live with an American family was a good cultural experience in the United States. I developed a very good relationship with her since I am an easy going person.

Mrs. Lyons' house was close to everything. As for accommodation, I was so lucky to have a full furnished room in a house with television, cable, and a dishwasher. Mrs. Lyons was always very open, generous, and communicative. She also helped me wash my clothes and always gave me a gift. She cared about me a lot and I felt fortunate to have her as a landlord and neighbor. Her positive behavior helped me spend a good academic year in Orono, Maine. I learned also about myself and my relationship with people. However, I had few friends.

As a Haitian, I became an ambassador in Orono, Maine. That is I felt like I represented Haiti and the black community as well. I observed in school that some people of color were very loud. I was aware of this bad stereotype and committed myself not to be too loud as a black male, since I especially lived in a house with a white woman. When I woke up, I took a shower, dressed nicely, wore cologne, and walked slowly in order not to bother her. "After Louisket is Louisket," said the beautiful white woman, meaning she didn't believe that she would find another tenant like me. She added that some folks warned her that I might exhibit negative behavior in her house. "But now everybody likes you Louisket." I was happy to learn that my behavior was acceptable. Mrs. Lyons made a party for me by inviting some professors from the University of Maine and her relatives. Her cousin Janet Lombardo drove from Massachusetts to Maine in order to cook for the party. It was the first time since I came to the United States that I found people so friendly as though I was with friends in Haiti. I am proud today to have some pictures to show the world. Haitian folks will understand the American people better after reading about my experience in this great country. American I met care about the world and want everyone to succeed. **Here are the pictures:**

Picture of Mrs. Lyons and me in her house in Maine

This is Professor Essivi on my right, me,
and Mrs. Lyons on my left at UMO

**This is Mrs. Lombardo on my right, me,
and Mrs. Lyons' aunt on my left in Maine**

This is me in Little Hall, University of Maine in Orono, Maine

This is Mrs. Lombardo and me

This is me and Prof. Gudrun in Maine

Dr. Smith on my right, me, and Dr. Gisele on my right in Maine

Mrs. Lombardo on my left, me,
and Dr. Slott on my right in Maine

This is me in the house of Mrs. Lyons in Maine

This is me and Mrs. Lyons, a great American woman

**This is me and other graduate students
at the University of Maine**

After my graduation at the University of Maine, I escorted a group of American students from the University of Maine to Quebec City, Canada with Dr. Jane Smith, French graduate coordinator and professor Essivi Abotsi, a colleague who is from Togo, Africa. I had the privilege of working with both of them while living in Canada. We used the Laval University campus to teach French to our students during our time in Quebec City. Students exposed to the French language outside of class, and they participated in various educational projects as well. We also went to explore a lot of aesthetic buildings and interesting urban planning. I personally had a great time in Quebec with all my students and colleagues. I also met some new people from all around the world before coming back to Orono, Maine.

Today once again I want to tell my brothers-in-law, if they think the best way to survive in this country is to stay away from school, my success is their answer. I knew for a fact that I was far from perfect as a human being, but since I left my brothers-in-law behind in Florida. I received so much love cross the USA. Now nobody can tell me that it is impossible for people of color to earn a degree here, no matter how poor they are or where they come from.

While I was in Maine, I provided interpretation assistance for many Haitian clients on the staff of the Farm Workers Unit of Pine Tree Legal Assistance (PTLA). I worked with Eric Nelson, Directing Attorney of the Farm Workers Unit in Bangor, Maine. My duties as a contractor included written and verbal translation, communication with Creole-speaking workers and other client-related activities under the supervision of Farm Workers Unit Attorney, Mike Guare. I enjoyed helping my fellow Haitians for the first time since I moved to the United States. "Our job is to live as well and as long as we can, and to help others to do the same," said former president Clinton in his book, which is titled "My Life."

In an instance I can share my sorrow in Haiti, and joy and excitement in the United States. In my opinion, Haitian teachers had too much power over their students. Students could not approach their teachers outside of class with questions, while in the United States it is totally different. Generally the Haitian teachers are used a teaching strategy which out of date based more on hold would be theory than practice. That is to say they believed students needed to memorize everything by heart otherwise they punished by their teachers. Whereas, in the United States of America, teachers knew this is an ineffective method. I found the teachers friendly enough with students even if they didn't prepare their assignments. American teachers understand the practical and the modern theories. They teach and wait until every student understands before moving to a new chapter. I definitely prefer the American system, which all modern research has shown to work better for most students.

Minorities in Haiti and in the USA

My experiences in Haiti and in the USA can be educational for those who were born in a wealthy country and never traveled outside of their countries to understand more of the world. They could also help, the American, Canadian or European immigrants to understand that they are not in their countries and must follow the rules of their new lands, which are vital for a world of peace.

Who is in the White House? President Barack Obama, his father is from Kenya and today the American people have made him the commander in chief in the Unites States of America. That means a lot not only to my son Ludgi Louisket, but also to all children of immigrants who are born in the United States of America and represent a wide variety of nations, cultures, languages, and religions. In order words, the United States of America is a country of opportunity where foreigners' children can become and do anything. It is the diversity in the USA which makes it one nation under God.

The 38th Governor of California, Arnold Schwarzenegger, actor, model, businessman, politician, is another good example for aliens who move to live the American dream. He is a native of Austria who serves this great nation. The Unites States is not the only country that gives minorities and aliens a chance to grow. Its neighbor Canada has made history too with Michaelle Jean, a Haitian-Canadian journalist who has become the first black Governor General in Canada.

My fellow immigrants, we are in these countries for a reason and of course we experience special challenges to adapt to a new culture. However, these good examples who came from different generations, cultures, and countries have been working entirely to change the world.

We should be inspired by them and get our kids to research them. The Canadian and American people welcome all immigrants whatever their faith they want us to succeed and do it with mutual respect. Let's not live up to negative stereotypes in these countries. Let's not disappoint people like Senator Ted Kennedy who worked overtime in the American Congress to help us live this dream today with our family members. Let's commit ourselves not to commit any crimes in the most powerful country on the earth. One of the best ways to do that is to go back to school to get good jobs and to stay off the streets. We need to stand up and work together with the American, Canadian, French people, etc. for peace in the world. If we follow my advice, if we change our neighborhoods with better education, we will make immigration reform easier for the Congress this year especially in the United States, so that undocumented immigrants will become eligible to live legally and support their sisters and brothers who are in desperate need in their countries.

In this world, I am not in a position to criticize anybody, not even my brothers-in-law who were taught that American teachers were unfair to minority students. Today again I want to tell them, they were wrong. It may be hard work but best way to survive in this country is to get a good education. Since I left my brothers-in-law in Florida, I received so much love and support in the USA. I completed two majors in French and Spanish literature and a Masters in Education. I inspired so many children in this country with my teaching style in different schools, and now nobody can lie to me about the American system.

Haitian's survivors on Jan 12, 2010

On my last night in Maine, I left Mrs. Lyons' house and went to visit my friend Timothy Allen, in blue bell. We had a great time together. One of the things I liked best about Maine was the people. I felt really sad when I left them. But I have a lot of good memories, which will have to do, since I don't know when I will see them again.

I moved to Barkhamsted, Connecticut to meet Nagena, love of my life with two beautiful children and prepare for the academic year 2009-2010. I accepted a teaching position in Connecticut shortly after returning from Quebec City to Maine. I was very impressed by world language department staff who welcomed me the day I came for my interview. I fell in love with this great team same day, and one of the assistant principals gave me a tour of the High School along with the Middle School in Regional 7 in Winsted, Connecticut. She talked to me nicely and introduced me to different teachers. I felt like I was in the State of Maine once again.

On January 12, 2010 I was in the Middle Regional School giving a lecture about Haiti. When I went back to my house, I went to bed and took a nap. I woke up around six in the evening to prepare for my classes the following morning, and I turned on the computer. I tried to find some information about Haiti as usual on Yahoo and read about an earthquake, which happened a few minutes earlier while I was sleeping. I knew for fact a lot of people would be affected because one of the Haitian schools collapsed in Petion-ville while I was studying in Maine and many innocent children cried out trapped inside of the building for days and died later. I knew the new crisis would be worse because Haitians do require any engineers or licenses to build houses in the island, so we have many bad constructions. Where are the Haitian authorities? Where are the building codes?

I felt depressed, like life didn't make any sense to me. I kept calling my sister Ifrancia who went to visit our family members in Haiti and there was no communication for weeks. I went to bed, but I couldn't sleep. I thought not only about my sister, cousins, aunts, uncles, friends, Haitian children who were sleeping on the streets, or lost their parents with everything, but also about the dead bodies in my homeland. I tried not to be ignorant; too many people from different nations got killed by this catastrophic earthquake because they were in Haiti to help my fellow Haitians. For example, Caribbean Islanders, Americans, Canadians, and Europeans were among the people who lost their lives on January 12, 2010. The same night, I figured out what to do to help rebuild my motherland since the challenge ahead is the responsibility of all of us. As a native of Haiti, I could not stay here in the United States not do anything. If I knew how to dance like Michael Jackson, I would do it or offer the world a CD if I could sing, in order to build schools for the ordinary children in my country. What I came up after many hours of thinking in this difficult time was to write about my experiences in Haiti and in the Unites States. One of my biggest challenges was to begin writing and decide which language to use. Obviously, I should begin with the strongest one since I spoke four. I wrote eight pages in French, but I said to myself that I was surrounded by many people who did not speak French, and they might not be able to understand my story. Indeed, I lived in a country where most of my potential readers spoke English. Finally, I decided not to continue writing in French, but in the English language. Here is the first thing that I wrote in French on January 12, 2010 at eleven fifteen at night:

Haiti my Motherland

What is happing to your children today?

Why have they tears all the time?

Why? Why have so many people died?

It's not alright, but the world is with us this time

It's alright. This is not a war, but a natural disaster

It's alright. Our future will be better

Have hope

Survivors wait for the future

Homeless be patient, housing will be built not in the capital

Children on the streets wait for schools

Don't cry

We love you

We love you

Don't cry

I began writing the same day because I couldn't sleep and I was so concerned about the future of Haitian survivors especially the ordinary children who lost their love ones. I had become a thinker and wanted to dedicate my time and energy in order to create something to help. As a native of Haiti I cared about what was happening in my homeland. Shortly after the catastrophic earthquake, I received so many emails from faculty members and staff at Temple University, University of Maine, Michigan State University, and Northwestern Regional High school, in Winsted, Connecticut.

It was totally impossible to get through to relatives for weeks in Haiti. Family members and friends kept calling me at midnight; nobody wanted to sleep. I got good news from my brother-in-law that my sister Ifrancia was alive. But my dear Celiane Romulus, a friend and aunt who used to support me when I was in the middle school in the Capital died, shortly after the earthquake, and her husband Jean Martin was unable to bury her body since there were too many dead bodies in the capital. My aunt Michelle Exume and her children have been living on the streets. Most of my neighbors died in their houses. My advisor Jean Lochard lost three children and four other relatives. Each time I called, I got more bad news and it hurt. I stop calling if I can't send money to fellow Haitians.

"Louisket come to my office," said one of the vice principals from Northwestern Regional School in Winsted, Connecticut. She said we belonged to a great community. All students and staff wanted to help me. I thought at the time nobody could imagine what I was feeling, too much death in my country, too many dead people whether they were my biological family members, or just human beings. In this difficult time, the people of my school have already raised and given me for my family and friends in Haiti $2,200.

I believe until now that we are a united family the Islanders at Northwestern Regional School, of course, and that's why we are teaching in the same institution. I sent the money to my relatives and friends in Haiti by Western Union and Money gram companies. They didn't charge me any fees for Haiti since those companies care about what happened to my homeland on Jan 12, 2010. It is a wonderful gesture by my fellow islanders, and I will be thankful to them for the rest of my life. They helped me feed more than forty five Haitians in need at the time. I am also proud of myself, If I did not study for many years to learn from American professors, today I wouldn't have the opportunity to give back what I learned nor be able to feed those Haitians either.

Unfortunately Haiti has become infamous once again for more than 270,000 Haitian bodies and dead foreigners who went to support the Haitian people. It is too late to remember the slavery; it is way too late. It is time to reconcile with each other and overcome the past. It is too long ago to remember the past, but too early to forget about thousands of human beings who were buried without coffins. It is too early to forget about a hundred thousand people who are homeless and currently living on the streets. This is a problem for all humanity I believe.

Think about Darlene Etienne, a sixteen year old girl who was pulled out by the French rescuers fifteen days after the quake. She didn't eat anything, didn't drink anything, but God saved her life. Sadly, a medical student named David, lived in the rubble for about three days in Carrefour, a few miles away from the Haitian Capital. His neighbors heard his cry and rescued him. He didn't ask to be president, senator, representative, but just for a cup of water and died shortly after drinking the water.

I was inspired by thousands of people who lost their lives in my homeland and hundreds of thousand of others who currently live on the streets. I never imagined that could happen to my motherland that I love so much. I don't think that I am a writer, but not trying is not an option in this difficult time. I am thankful for the enthusiasm of my students and faculty as well as the support of my mother-in-law Marie-Carmelle, and father-in-law Neige. This is my first book despite of the publication of several poems at Temple University.

I wish to express my gratitude to my family members and friends who helped me while I was busy of writing: Toussaint Louverture, Ifrancia, Jony, Kettelie, Judette, ponoch, Stanley Edmond, Geenaelle, Dr. Smith, Prof. Essivi, Dr. Thomas Morton, Prof. Maria Cruz, Dr. Roget, Dr. Laura, Prof. Grégoire Rosia, Prof. Hakim, Dr. Lucner, Prof. Judithe, Natalie, Haniel, Benson, Clark, Fanfanze, Tony, Raoul, Daniel, Michel, Lucien, Soleine, Ugin, Saintalia, Felder, Ilorian, Tenemba, Vilcean, Vilcida, Sainthérèse, Paulma, Salonise, Jeanine, vania, Naomi, Dalice, Hermithe, Naoline, Roseline, Osette, Pierre-Louis, Jeanty, Hubert, Ginette, Ganette, Gilvert, Daniel, Jean Bony, Eliassaint, Ruthe, Osny, Olguine, Mirold, Sonithe, Marie-Rosemithe, Serné, Waselet, Marie-Carmelle, Rachelle, Rebecca, Anrio, Amos, Aniel, Pirkol, Nazaire, Nicole, Chalisna, Manouche, Edeline, Marie-Paule, Marc-Henry, Mickelson, Miriam, Michel-ange, Michigan, Fanila, Imanues, Semilda, Markenf, Junior, Mercimise, Mercina, Paul Jean Mario, Nadège, Madochée, Betie, Hervie, Nahom, Guyrlene, Fara, Nandie, Sonithe, Rosemithe, Rosemonde, Louna, Clarice, Frantz, Magrelitha, Mesguerre, Valerie, Vilaire, Junie, Michecat, Sonithe, Ilfaut, Ernest, Ernithe, Francia, Dumassais, Colin, Ketia, Fifi, Vania, Apolos, Laguerre, Luckner, Sandy, Adam, Lochard and his family, inspector Andre, Jean Joseph Filostin, Regente, Père Lamour, Jean Louis Néus, venette, Rivelineau, Paul Pierre, Islanders, Gomez, Elnie Goodman, Excellent Petion, Acélia, Mirtha, Harry Denis, Marie-Michel Exumé, Chantale, Alexandra, Liberata, and all members of the Haitian diaspora.

On behalf of the Haitian people, I want to thank President Barack Obama and his wife for helping our fellow citizens shortly after the earthquake and asking two former Presidents of the United States of America Clinton and Bush to raise money for Haiti. The challenge we face on the island of Hispaniola today would require everyone to do something in order to save lives. This is not a right or left issue. That's right I also want to thank former Presidents Clinton and Bush for accepting to work for the Haitian people, Vice President Joe Biden and his wife, Secretary Hilary Clinton, former first lady Laura Bush, Senator John Kerry, Senator John MacCain, Former Governor Sarah Palin, Chairman Steele Michael, President House Representative Nancy Pelosi, Prime Minister Stephen Harper, General Governor Michaelle Jean, Brazilian President Luiz Inacio Lula da Silva, Dominican President Leonel Fernandez, French President Nicolas Sarkozy, former president Nelson Mandela, Attorney General Eric Holder, Secretary of Defense Robert Gates, Secretary of Homeland Security Janet Napolitano, Secretary of Health and Human Services Kathleen Sebelius, Former secretary Colin Power, and Condoleezza, U.S. Ambassador Susan Rice, Rev. Jesse Jackson, Rev. Al Sharpton, Percy Sutton, Barbara Jordon, Daniel James, Chair Veronica L. Turner, and all Stars in the world like, Stanley F. and Fiona B. Druckenmiller, John M. Templeton, William H (Bill) III and Melinda F. Gates, Michael R. Bloomberg, Oprah, Lionel Richie, Wyclef Jean, Angelina Jolie, Brad Pitt, Chris Brown, Madonna, Justin Timberlake, Chris Martin, Charles Aznavour, Youssou N. Dour, Gisele Bundchen, George Clooney, Vanessa Baker, Nelly Furtado, Hollywood Foreign Press association, Larry King, Red cross, Telethon, Unicef, American Airlines, Doctors without Borders, the inter-America Court of Human Rights, based in Costa Rica who never abandoned the Haitian people and all countries that gave donations to Haiti in order to save lives in my homeland.

In addition, I am grateful to Father Pierre Lebeller, and Brother Balde Arnold who helped me become a real citizen while I was growing up in Haiti. I am also grateful to Dr. Abdul who is currently teaching at Michigan State University in Michigan, and Tanisha Broadnax, coordinator of Nursing program at the University of Pennsylvania. They both dedicated their time to help me succeed in this long project.

After the earthquake, the Haitian people did not know what to do, they cried for help for all Haitian earthquake victims, dead family members, the hungry and homeless, Western Union company, CVS, Walt-mart, Money Gram, CAM, and thousands of others companies and individuals heard the voice of our fellow Haitians by allowing anyone to send money to Haiti without taxes and I want to thank them as well.